1000 Best Quick and Easy Time-Saving Strategies

JAMIE NOVAK

SOURCEBOOKS, INC.®
NAPERVILLE, ILLINOIS

Copyright © 2007 by Jamie Novak
Cover and internal design © 2007 by Sourcebooks, Inc.
Cover photo © Sumaya/2005
Internal illustration © Art Explosion
Sourcebooks and the colophon are registered trademarks of Source-
books, Inc.

Published by Sourcebooks, Inc.
P.O. Box 4410, Naperville, Illinois 60567-4410
(630) 961-3900
Fax: (630) 961-2168
www.sourcebooks.com

Library of Congress Cataloging-in-Publication Data

Novak, Jamie.
  1000 best quick and easy time-saving strategies / Jamie Novak.
    p. cm.
  Includes index.
  ISBN-13: 978-1-4022-0919-2
  ISBN-10: 1-4022-0919-3
  1. Time management. 2. Self-management (Psychology) I. Title. II.
Title: One thousand best quick and easy time-saving strategies.

BF637.T5N68 2007
640'.43--dc22

                                        2006038958

        Printed and bound in the United States of America.
              LB 10 9 8 7 6 5 4 3 2 1

Dedicated To

You! The person who didn't plan for things to turn out exactly like this: feeling overwhelmed, stressed-out, always behind with a to-do list a mile long and no time for the fun stuff in life. I want to help you catch your breath so you can have more time to focus on the important things, because you realize this is not a dress rehearsal—this is your one shot to live a life you love.

And to Sue Novak, my mother and best friend, who taught me much of what I know about time management and whose sudden passing showed me just how important it is to live without regrets and to make the most of every moment I am given.

Contents

Acknowledgments

A huge thank you to my editor Bethany Brown, my publicist Whitney Lehman, and the entire Sourcebooks team, including Ewurama Ewusi-Mensah, Stephanie Wheatley, and Rachel Jay. You are each extremely talented, and I thank you for bringing enthusiasm and your special creative touch to my book. I am blessed to be able to work with you.

Also many thanks to my outstanding agent, Jessica Faust of BookEnds. You have a gift for matching authors with projects that showcase their talents, and I am honored to be working with you.

To each of you who supports my work and allows me to share my gift with you, thank you for seeing my vision and for helping me spread the word. I have you to thank for the fact that I am able to wake up every morning and do a job that I love so much, I can hardly call it work! We may not have had the chance to meet in person yet, but I sincerely hope we will, as I already feel as though I know you. You hold a special place in my heart.

Introduction

Thanks for picking up my book. Right off the bat, let me tell you that this time-management book is very different from all the other books out there on this subject. How is it different, you ask? Well, to start with, you will not find any graphs to fill out, charts to track your progress, or exercises to do. Quite honestly, if you had time to do all that, you probably wouldn't need to read this book!

Instead, I wrote this book to share my revolutionary approach with you; it is filled with time-management tips as flexible as your ever-changing schedule. I've simply given you the best of the best tips and ideas that *really* work in the real world. These are the same tips I've taught for years and the ones I use myself, so they are proven to work wonders. I've been working with busy people, lots of them families, for over fifteen years, so I know you are not alone in your struggle to manage time. I also know that you cannot sit down and read this book cover-to-cover. On most days I bet you'll count yourself lucky if you can get in just half a page. This is perfect since this book is best read tip-by-tip, not cover-to-cover. Just like my first book in this series, *1000 Best Quick and Easy Organizing Secrets*, this book is portable, and it cuts to the chase with tips that are realistic.

I promise that you'll only find practical ideas here. I know you are busy, so I won't waste your time with solutions that simply do not work or take too much time and effort to implement and maintain. If you have tried other time-management methods before—bought books, journals, and calendars, or even attended seminars—you may have gotten some good ideas here and there. But I've pulled together the very best ideas and laid them out in a way that you can read quickly and implement immediately for instant results. So, if you are looking for quick fixes that last a lifetime, you're in the right place. I invite you to join me as we figure out how to solve your time crisis once and for all!

Before we begin, I want to assure you that there is hope! I'm sure, since you are reading this book, that your life is not going exactly how you planned, which means you may be feeling a little (or a lot) frustrated. You probably have less control over your time than you would like. You may be busy all day, but things still don't seem to be getting done. Are you short on patience? Are you missing the important stuff in life? Are you just plain sick and tired of rushing around and feeling overwhelmed? If this is the case, then you are in the right place. The good news is that no matter what situation you are in—whether you have struggled with time your whole life or whether this is a new issue due to a recent change in your life—starting today, you can gain control over your time and you will see changes immediately!

Do you need more time? If so, you are like so many of us who find ourselves running around day after day in a whirlwind: rushed, behind, overworked, stressed-out, and short on patience; living every day jam-packed with things we *have* to do with not enough time to do the things we want to do! Sound familiar? If it does, this book is for you.

The most important thing to know, as we begin this journey to recover your time, is that you cannot manage your time. All you can do is manage yourself. If you've been struggling to get a handle on your time, you've been fighting a losing battle. No wonder it never worked out! I'm going to show you how to manage *you*. Once you learn how to do that, life gets a whole lot easier.

I am not here to tell you how to spend your time, not here to tell you to work harder and smarter, not here to push you to get more done. I am here to show you how to figure out what needs to get done and what you want to get done (the fun stuff)—and then how to get it done with less stress.

Lastly, let me assure you that I've been there, too. I have days that by the end of them I'm exhausted but still have not crossed anything off my to-do list. Email, junk mail, and people who are a tad too chatty can overwhelm me. And yes, I have been known to procrastinate, and I, too, feel bad having to decline invitations. I don't want you to think that I have all the time in the world and can't relate, because that's just not true. Just like you, some days I feel like I need more time. We're all in the same rush-and-hurry boat, but you can jump ship. I struck a balance and have found simple ways to manage myself. If you have a dream that keeps getting put on hold or if you simply want to feel less rushed, these tips are guaranteed to help you create a life you love.

Ready? Let's go! I want you to feel less stressed starting today!

P.S. A little fine print before we get going: In this fast-paced world, contact information can sometimes change. At the time this book was written, all the contact information provided for various resources and companies throughout this book was current. I apologize in advance if any of the information has changed since the time this book was printed. If you'd like to report a change so we can update future printings, please do so at www.jamienovak.com.

I've included website addresses and other company contact information in this book for products and services that you may want to check out. I am not affiliated with these companies; I just love to share information on helpful products and services whenever I come across them. Now on to the good stuff!

HOW TO USE THIS BOOK

I promise this book is to-the-point and immediately useful since I know if you had time to read a book cover-to-cover on time management, you wouldn't need one!

So, where should you start? I'd strongly suggest you read part one first; it will give you all the basics on time management. After that, it's your call. Turn to the section that best meets your needs at this time. Go directly to meal planning if that is your biggest challenge right now, but if papers or photos are costing you time, then start there. The choice is yours; you can't do it wrong. And if you are just overwhelmed by it all and the thought of picking a section is one decision too many, then read the tips in order.

Many readers of my first book in this series, *1000 Best Quick and Easy Organizing Secrets*, reported that they carried a pad of sticky notes along with the book. That way, when they wanted to mark a tip, they could pop a note on the page and could even write a note to themselves. You might try doing the same thing.

This book is so portable that you can tuck it into your briefcase or diaper bag, so that whenever you have a spare moment you can read just one or two more tips.

Not all of the one thousand strategies will work for you since there are no cookie-cutter solutions and no two time challenges are the same. But most of them *will* work for you, and many can be modified to suit your lifestyle.

Once you read the book, I encourage you to keep it on your bookshelf as a reference. Certain sections, like holidays, vacation, and new baby, may not apply to you right now. But they may at some point, so hold onto the book and pull it out as needed for a refresher. Most people report that having the book on hand and reading a tip or two every now and then gives them even more inspiration; they have also found the resource sections quite helpful.

I'm so excited that you are taking control of your time, and I'm wishing all good things for you as you start living the life of your dreams!

Part One:

Setting Up for Success

Most of us can manage a new routine for a few days or even a few weeks. But soon that new routine is forgotten, and all too quickly we are back to our old ways. This usually happens for one of two reasons. One, you are not convinced of the payoff, so you lose interest. Or two, the new way is not easy, and since we are so busy, we desperately need easy. The good news is that all my solutions are easy, so that's not going to be an issue. But I also want you to be wildly excited about the payoff. By that I mean that I want you to be clear about why you want to make changes in how you manage time. Once you know *why*, it gets much easier to stick with new routines.

The first thing we'll do is figure out what's not working for you, learn what is working for you, and determine why you want to make changes. Then we'll move on to the ten golden rules. All that will jump-start your success, and I want you to be successful! So let's get started together.

QUICK QUIZ: ASSESSING THE DAMAGE

1. How often do you volunteer to do something or help someone *without* being asked? C

   A. almost never B. sometimes C. most of the time

2. How often are there items left undone on your to-do list at the end of the day? C

   A. almost never B. sometimes C. most of the time

3. How often do you waste time chatting about nothing, gossiping, or watching TV shows you don't really like? B

   A. almost never B. sometimes C. most of the time

4. How often do you pick up the phone just because it rings, even if you are in the middle of something? A

   A. almost never B. sometimes C. most of the time

5. How often do you spend time looking for lost or misplaced things like your keys, cell phone, pieces of paper, etc.? C

   A. almost never B. sometimes C. most of the time

6. How often do you put off tasks, planning to get back to them later? C

   A. almost never B. sometimes C. most of the time

7. How often do you feel overwhelmed, like you don't have enough time? C

   A. almost never B. sometimes C. most of the time

8. How often do you honk (or want to honk) at the car in front of you as soon as a red light turns green? B

   A. almost never B. sometimes C. most of the time

9. How often do you arrive late (or just in the nick

of time) for appointments? *C*

    A. almost never B. sometimes C. most of the time

10. How often do you end up doing a task someone else could do just because you are sure
you can do it better or faster? *C*

    A. almost never B. sometimes C. most of the time

11. How often are you guilted into volunteering? *B*

    A. almost never B. sometimes C. most of the time

12. How often do you have to move mail or piles of
papers off your countertop or table at home to
use the space? *B*

    A. almost never B. sometimes C. most of the time

13. How often do you notice that your heels and
elbows are in need of a little lotion? *C*

    A. almost never B. sometimes C. most of the time

14. How often do you try to remember everything
you need to do in your mind instead of writing
out a to-do list? *C*

    A. almost never B. sometimes C. most of the time

MOSTLY A'S: YOU COULD HAVE WRITTEN THIS BOOK

You are a time-management guru. You have mastered the art of juggling routines, balancing schedules, and setting boundaries. You can delegate like a pro, and you feel good about all you accomplish. You have the opposite challenge of most people; you need to learn how to pace yourself and take enough time for you, while showing others how to be self-sufficient and remembering that your way of doing things is not the only way. This book will serve as a guide for you to learn how to involve others in your plan. You'll feel great as you read the tips and see how much you are already doing, and you'll pick up some fantastic new ideas you can implement immediately.

MOSTLY B'S: GOT IT TOGETHER SOME DAYS, HOLDING ON BY A THREAD OTHER DAYS

Some days you've got it together, and other days...not so much. You are trying hard and succeeding most of the time. It is important for you to focus on all that you *do* accomplish since you are doing more than you may think. Stop and give yourself credit, then craft a plan for getting a better handle on your to-do list. Watch out so you don't get sidetracked by the zigzag. Your best bet it to choose one area you'd like to improve and work on that until you master it before moving on. This book will be your guide. Focus on the areas of the book that will make the most significant change quickly.

MOSTLY C'S: STOP THE WORLD, I WANT TO GET OFF

You feel completely overwhelmed most days, but the good news is that there is hope! Sure you may run late, feel stressed-out, run around putting out fires, and zigzag through your day. You may also suffer from low energy and just want the world to stop so you can catch up. I can assure you that you are not alone. Slow down, figure out your priorities, and craft a simple plan to regain control over your time and life. This book will be a reference for you for life. Go through the book slowly, following all the steps, and within a matter of days you will see positive changes. The key for you is going to be getting started. Don't let this book sit unread on a pile in your house. Carry it with you, and use it daily.

1.

The Basics of the Ten Golden Rules

1. <u>Take responsibili</u>ty. Realize that you alone are responsible for your time and how you use it. Sure, there are some times when things are truly out of our control. But the majority of the time, you do have a say. So, be a ruthless gatekeeper and do not allow your time to be stolen. If it helps, pretend each of your 1,440 minutes a day is a dollar, and think before you spend that money.

2. Wear a watch. Wearing a watch all day long will vastly improve your ability to gauge time. Plus, you will always know what time it is, and knowing that helps to keep you on track, avoiding those last-minute, "how did it get so late" moments when you have to rush. Note: If you are not a big fan of wearing a watch, you can still have a clock close at hand by opting for a small version that hangs from your belt loop, purse, diaper bag handle, or some other creative version.

3. Use a timer. This is not to suggest you should become so regimented that a bell sounds a few times an hour. But a simple buzz can remind you it is time to get ready to leave or to start dinner or to make that phone call.

4. Time yourself. Time yourself doing routine tasks, not so that you can compress your routine and do it faster, but so that you can accurately set aside enough time in the future. When you are not sure how long things take, you can easily over- or underestimate how much time you need. This can put you behind schedule or cause you not to start a task because you think it will take longer than it really does.

5. Do the complete job the first time. When you only do half a job, your to-do list becomes much longer since there is also other work waiting for your attention. For example, when a meal is complete you or someone else should get the dishes in the dishwasher right away or if you are the dishwasher, wash them.

6. Pay attention. We can be so rushed that we do things without being fully aware and later can't remember what we did, said, or where we left an item. For example, if you walk into the house talking on your cell phone and carrying the mail, you might toss your keys to the side. Then when you need them again, you won't remember where you left them. When you pay attention to what you are doing and adopt easy-to-remember routines, like always hanging your keys on the same hook when you come through the door, life gets easier.

7. Label everything. A label makes it quick and easy to locate items. Labels on shelves in the garage help you to find things easily; labels on laundry baskets help you to see quickly where to toss the whites. Color-coding is another easy way to identify things and people; for example, a white laundry basket for whites and a blue one for darks, or a green circle around events on the family calendar that require a child being taxied somewhere. Labels also deter us from tossing something in the wrong place, since the label reminds us exactly what does and *does not* belong there.

8. Store it where you use it. Place items you need in handy places. If you commonly read in the living room, then keep your magazines on the coffee table and not on your bedroom nightstand. Keep doubles of things, and store them where you use them. For example, if you use scissors in the kitchen to open boxes, then keep a kitchen pair in a drawer instead of always running to the home office to grab a pair off your desk.

9. Write it down in the right place the first time. This may appear to take more time, since you have to grab a pen and paper. But in actuality, it ends up saving you time. Once you write it down, you free up space in your mind so you have less mental clutter. Plus, you'll remember to do it. And please stop writing on the back of envelopes or on scraps of paper! Write in the right place the first time, like a *single* spiral notebook set aside just for your notes.

10. Rethink your word choices. Stop saying you have no time and that you are so busy. Remember, you believe what you hear, and if you hear yourself saying it, you will believe it. Instead, try reminding yourself that there is plenty of time for everything.

2.

"No" Is the Hardest Word to Say

11. Once you know what is important to you at this time in your life, it will be easier to decline offers that take you away from doing those things that matter to you. But saying "no" is often easier said than done. Just remember that for everything you say "yes" to, you are saying "no" to something else. If it helps, think of this equation: If I want to add X to my schedule, I need to subtract Y.

12. Saying "no" can truly be difficult. You don't want to disappoint another person, and we are taught to be helpful. But learning to say "no," at least some of the time, means you are recognizing your own need for time, and that is exactly what you need to learn how to do.

13. Practice declining offers (a more palatable term for saying "no"). The more you do it, the easier it will become. Even if you have to practice out loud in the shower, the more often you say it, the more comfortable it becomes.

14. Be an equal opportunity decliner. Don't just decline social engagements and requests to volunteer your time. Also give yourself permission to decline offers from family members and close friends to do favors or spend time on things that are not really high on your list of priorities.

15. Have a policy in place. Decide ahead of time how many social engagements a month you want to accept, how many hours you want to spend on volunteer activities, and how often you are willing to watch other people's children. Once you know your magic number, you can agree up to that point and then simply state your policy. People are less likely to argue with you or become insulted by your refusal when you blame it on a policy.

16. Post your policy! Just having a policy is not enough—you need write it out and refer to it often until you have committed it to memory. Try posting the policy by your phone and calendar to serve as a visual reminder that can be extremely helpful until you are in the habit of declining gracefully.

17. Keep in mind that you can't do it all and still do it all well. Stop spreading yourself too thin and disappointing people or not doing your best work.

18. Think of the return you will get on your investment of time before you agree to take on a task. You need time to do the more important tasks that accomplish your goals; don't do the things that give little or no return.

19. When in doubt, say "no" now. You can always go back and say "yes" later. It is much easier that way than to accept and have to bow out down the road.

20. When you are stuck in a situation where you are being asked to do something that you do not want to do, simply ask the person making the request to check with you about it later. This allows you an escape and the time to think it through.

21. When you are asked to volunteer, before you jump in and say "yes," ask questions about what will be required of you. For example, how much time did the last person who did this job spend working on the project? Once you know that, you will better be able to make your decision to accept or decline.

22. Compromise. If you are asked to be the program chairperson, for instance, compromise and agree to be a co-chair but not the lead. You do have negotiating power when being asked for your assistance.

23. Stop volunteering. Often, without even being asked, we jump in and offer to help—which translates into more work for us. Wait until you are asked—it can save you lots of time.

24. If you plan on volunteering for one of a number of available tasks, sign up first so you can be sure to get the task that best suits your skills, is most fun for you, or that will take the least amount of time. You do have a choice about how you spend your time.

25. Don't forget that always doing for others can seriously affect your quality of life. It is wonderful to be generous with your time, but only after you have taken care of things in your own life. Doing for others before you do for yourself is not in anyone's best interest.

26. Be sure to share your new plan with friends and family members, so they are not insulted when you suddenly start to decline invitations. Avoid assuming how they are going to react; you might feel nervous broaching the subject because you are fearful that they will be upset or will make you feel guilty. Instead, most people report that friends and family agree that they too are overwhelmed and welcome the idea of cutting back. Be sure to compromise; for example, instead of weekly trips to the mall, go window-shopping once a month and get together on one other day to run errands.

27. Don't allow others to take advantage of you. Sometimes when we offer to help, we get sucked into much more than we expected. It is okay to step up and say you can only give so much more time before you have to move on to your next activity, or whatever the case may be.

28. A great way to buy yourself time when you are on the spot is to say you have to check with your family. This allows you time to think it over before committing or declining.

29. Simply decline the offer but agree to help them find someone else. Sometimes locating a volunteer is less time-consuming than volunteering yourself. You can qualify this by saying you'd be willing to check with three friends.

30. Always remember that if you have agreed to something, you *always* have the right to rescind your offer. You can simply say that after looking at your schedule you can't possibly fit it in right now. This is a better option for everyone involved, you'd never be able to do your best when you're under pressure.

31. Take a moment to ask yourself why you are always volunteering, because there is always a reason. Do you have a strong desire to please? Do you enjoy the praise? Once you know the reason, you can look for other ways to get that same result. Maybe instead of heading up an organization, you can ask for some feedback on the meals you cook at home. The compliments you get may feed your need and help you to pass up other opportunities.

32. Keep the ball out of your court; don't offer to return the call or organize the event. Instead, put the onus on someone else to do the follow-up—this alone can save you lots of time.

3.

Your Plan and Getting Started

33. What will you do with the time you find by better managing your day? Knowing the answer to that question will motivate you to make changes in the way that you choose to use your time. Take a moment to ask yourself that question and pin down one item that really gets you excited about managing your time. For example, you might want to spend more time with your children, join a book club, go out on dates with your spouse, or take a cooking class. Once you have identified one or two things that are important to you, you'll be much more inspired to make the necessary changes and keep them in place.

34. How is your life affected by the fact that you don't have enough time? Are you stressed-out, not sleeping well, not sleeping enough, distracted, or impatient? Once you know the cost of not having enough time, you'll find yourself even more motivated to gain control over your day.

35. Where do you need more time? Take a moment and think about the areas of your life. Where do you always feel rushed? Some of us just need more time all day long! But most of us have trouble managing just one or two specific areas of our lives. You might be rushed to get out the door in the morning or you might find it difficult to leave work on time or you might need more time with your family in the evening or want to reclaim your weekends. There are solutions for every area of your life, but identifying one or two specific time challenges will help you know where to start to make the most meaningful and dramatic change in your life.

36. Where are you wasting time? Notice where you tend to lose time throughout your day. It might be a search and rescue mission to find your keys before you can walk out the door or walking out the door without everything you need and then having to waste time running back inside. Or you might be losing time checking emails, sifting through mail, or stopping at the store for the third time in the same week because you forgot to buy everything the first time. Identifying where you lose time is the first step towards recouping it.

37. Almost more important than figuring out what is not working is taking note of what is working. Once you know that, you can duplicate it in other areas. Take notice of the times during the day when you grumble, "There has to be a better way," as well as when you say, "That was easy." Whenever something is working, it is usually because there is a simple system in place.

38. Who are you today? You and your interests are bound to change, so what you once found important and made time for may not be so important anymore. It is vital to figure out what is important to you at this time in your life. There are many stages in your life, and what was a priority a few years ago may no longer hold much interest for you now. No sense trying to find time to fit in the things that do not make you happy. Conversely, if something makes you very happy, then it is of the utmost importance to make the time for it.

39. Avoid the trap of planning for the future while missing the present. Let's say you hope to one day take cooking classes but can't pursue that interest today. Still, you find yourself clipping out information on cooking classes and spending time filing it away. You might even waste time shopping for cooking utensils and appliances that you will simply store away for possible future use. So what happens if between now and then you change your mind about taking the classes or the information you clipped and supplies you bought become outdated? You can't get back the time it took you to store the stuff and clean around it.

40. Rethink how you use your time at least every year. Sometimes we can get stuck in a rut and just continue doing something because we have always done it. Consider carefully how you spend your time, and make sure you are doing things that are important to you *now*.

41. You don't have enough time to do things that are just of interest to someone else; they need to be of interest to you as well. Sometimes you might find yourself watching a movie with your family even though it is not a movie you'd normally choose to watch, but that's not what I'm talking about. What I mean is getting roped into spending large quantities of time doing something just for someone else; if you are not doing it for the right reasons, you may end up resenting the whole situation.

42. Be sure that you genuinely like the people you are spending most of your time with. Life is short. Don't waste it in the company of people that you don't enjoy being around. While it's true that there are times you have to be around people that are not on your favorite-people list, there is also plenty of time to choose who you want to be around, so choose carefully.

43. If there is something that you want to do, then make time for it now. Don't wait! Having regrets is not comfortable. Make the time you need to accomplish the most important things to you and your family. And while we are on the subject, do you know what is important to your family? If you haven't asked lately, then it's time to check. You may be surprised by their answers.

44. When faced with a choice about how to spend your time, try asking yourself, "Six months from now, will I regret not doing this?" The answer can help bring some clarity to the situation.

45. Eliminate the word "should" from your vocabulary. When you say you should do something, it simply means that you are not convinced that you want to do it, and when you don't want to do something, you will tend to procrastinate about getting it done. Instead, say you *want* to do something or you *don't want* to do something. If it is something you don't want to do, figure out a way to let someone else do it or just buckle down and get it done. But stop trying to convince yourself you "should" do something.

46. Think about tasks from a new or different perspective. Just because something has always been done a certain way doesn't mean it always has to be done that way. In fact, it may not even be the best way. Think outside the box.

47. Craft a plan that will work for you. If you have two toddlers at home with you all day, then a plan that has you running the vacuum during naptime will not work. Take all relevant factors into consideration when creating your plan. Be flexible and keep in mind that whatever phase of life you are in right now will pass. So if you have three small children who have play dates at your home but you are expecting that there will never be toys in your living room, you are probably being unrealistic. In a few years, however, that may be a doable plan. Don't wish away whatever stage you are currently in, because it will be gone all too quickly.

48. Your plan has to be *your* plan. Not your spouse's plan and not your mother's plan, but yours and yours alone. If you are not committed to the plan, then it will not work. You must set yourself up to succeed, not fail!

49. Remember that there is no perfect plan for gaining control over your time. If the goals you set for yourself are too high, then you will never be able to meet your own expectations. So set the bar low, meet that goal, and move on.

50. If you start with small, achievable goals, then you can work on reaching one goal and then move on to the next. But if you have one huge goal, you will never want to start, since it will seem so overwhelming.

51. Keep in mind that there is no right or wrong plan. You can waste valuable time worrying if this is the right plan for you, but instead you should jump in and carry it out. The results will show you if it is the right plan or not. Then you can make adjustments. But looking at a plan on paper and trying to figure out if it is right for you is impossible. You have to try it on for size.

52. Plan for delays; that way when they happen, you will not be surprised or thrown off your timetable. Traffic, weather, and road construction are all examples of things that are out of your control, but you can control how you allow them to affect you. By planning for them, you gain time if they don't happen, and you stay on track if they do.

53. Don't be fearful that planning will dampen your ability to be spontaneous or creative. Rest assured that the exact opposite is true. When you have a plan, you save time—which means there will also be unscheduled time to use as you choose.

54. Fill your gas tank when it is half-empty instead of waiting until the gas light comes on, forcing you to add an unplanned stop in your day or worse, run out of gas and waste a whole lot of time.

55. Put a clock in the bathroom. This is extremely helpful when you only have ten minutes to squeeze in a shower or you know you tend to lose track of time while fussing with your hair or applying makeup.

56. Set your clocks with the correct time. Setting clocks ahead ten or fifteen minutes is an outdated trick that rarely works. Usually, we remember we set the clocks ahead and tend to automatically factor in the time difference when looking at the clock. Plus, if you only set some clocks ahead and leave others with the correct time, you are apt to be easily confused about which clock is right. You might end up running even later because you've mixed up the two.

57. Set your goal and work in reverse so you know what needs to be accomplished by when and so you will be on time. This reverse timeline idea works equally well for getting out the door in the morning as it does for a long-range project, such as a room remodel.

58. Calculate your own personal quotient. Say, for example, you have to be at the recreation center to register your child for soccer at 8:00 a.m. tomorrow morning. Here's how you'd do the calculations to determine your quotient:

Nighttime routine: You like to get eight hours of sleep, and it takes you fifteen minutes to fall asleep plus fifteen minutes to get ready for bed. Additionally, you'll need fifteen minutes to locate the registration form in the pile of papers on the kitchen counter.

Morning routine: It takes you forty-five minutes to get ready, then fifteen minutes for breakfast, and the recreation center is a five-minute drive without traffic or red lights, but you'll plan for fifteen minutes to be on the safe side.

59. To figure out what time you need to set your alarm for, do the calculations. It will take you one hour and fifteen minutes to get up and get there, so you need to be out of bed at 6:45 a.m. (If you tend to hit the snooze button, set the alarm for earlier.) In order to get eight hours of sleep the night before, you should be asleep by 10:45 p.m., and since it takes you a half hour to get ready and fall asleep, you should start getting ready for bed at 10:15 p.m. Before that, you'll need at least fifteen minutes to find the paperwork. Since it always takes longer than you expect, set aside a half hour; if you find it sooner you've got extra time. (It is not suggested that you look through the piles of papers right before getting ready for bed—seeing all those things you still need to do might distract you!)

60. Setting a timer is helpful to keep you focused and on track.

61. At the end of the day, remember that this is your life, and you alone have the power to control it. Stop complaining that time is getting away from you, and stop blaming others for stealing your time—that only wastes more time. Instead, take control and start using your time more wisely.

62. We can't manage time; we can only manage ourselves. So stop fighting a losing battle, and start focusing on your actions, not on the minutes in the day.

HAVE MORE TIME TODAY!

1. Start practicing the ten golden rules of time management.
2. Learn to say "no" gracefully and not feel guilty about it.
3. Create a plan that will work for your lifestyle.

TRY THIS:

Stop thinking that you don't have enough time. Instead, remind yourself that you have enough time to get the things done that you choose to do. You'll believe what you tell yourself. If you tell yourself you don't have enough time, that's true, but if you tell yourself there is time for everything important, then that becomes true.

REPEAT AFTER ME:

"I'd love to, but that's our family time. Thanks for thinking of me. I hope you can find someone."

Part Two:

Fitting It All In

The one question I get asked more than any other about time management is, "How do I prioritize my to-do list?" Trying to figure out what to do first on your to-do list is not the place to start. The place to start is to figure out what your priorities are. Once you know that you'll know what's first on your list. So you can stop arranging and rearranging your list; don't worry about assigning A's or 1's to your top tasks—all of that is a waste of time if you haven't identified what's important. Instead, pick the top three things that are most important to you, and do the tasks related to those first.

4.

Calendar/ Planner

63. Choose a calendar that is going to work for your life. Don't bother trying to get the newest gadget. If it is not right for you, then it is never going to work. Instead, set yourself up for success by choosing one that will work for you. (See page 45 to help you determine which calendar style is the best match for your lifestyle and personality.)

64. Blocking out your time is the first thing you need to do. There will never be left-over time for you to use to do the things you enjoy doing. Life is short. Put those things on the calendar first, then add everything else in around that. Use a pen to mark off date night with your spouse, book club, coffee with a friend, knitting class, hair appointments, and chunks of time with no agenda so you can allow spontaneity to return into your life.

65. Before you add a task or appointment onto your calendar, take a moment to be sure it matches up with your current priorities. If you don't, you'll end up dreading it and then pro-crastinating about getting it done.

66. You can even write your short list of pri-orities out on a sticky note and post it near your calendar. Use that list to decide how best to spend your time. Sometimes the work of prioritizing can feel overwhelming, like you have to sort out your entire life before you know what to do and what not to do. If thinking in terms of "yes" and "no" feels less complicated, then create that list: one column of things you will no longer accept, like chairing an organization, and another column of thing you will accept, like two play dates a week for your child.

67. Set par levels for different activities. For example, if you enjoy taking classes at the local adult community center, then you might find yourself torn about how many to cram into your schedule. Simplify the decision-making process by setting a par level, say three: you'll choose three classes to take per semester. You can also set par levels based on the number of hours or the cost. So, you might say you'll spend two Saturday nights a month out of the house socializing or you'll only attend three weddings per year since your budget only supports purchasing that many gifts.

68. Stick with a single calendar. Having more than one calendar confuses things more than having no calendar at all, since you'll have difficulty remembering to cross-reference them and you will inevitably double-book yourself.

69. Don't forget the "white space": it's a must. If you schedule your life with a series of back-to-back chores, errands, appointments, and tasks, you'll burn out very quickly. Instead, allow room for plenty of white space—chunks of time or entire days during which you have no obligations and can relax or just do what you feel.

70. Scheduling back-to-back appointments is also a bad idea since that does not leave you any buffer time between activities. You never know what can cause you to run late—a traffic jam, a sad child, having to get gas in the car, lost keys, inclement weather, construction, a chatty friend, or someone else running behind, which in turn puts you behind; any one of these or a myriad of other issues can cause you to fall behind. Leaving that buffer time allows you to quickly get back on track.

71. When you enter an item onto your calendar that requires other actions, make a note of those as well. For example, if you write down a birthday party on the calendar, go back a week or so and make a note to buy the gift and the card. This will help you avoid last-minute dashes to the store or running late that day because you have to shop on the way and wrap the gift in the car.

72. Write all the information related to the event on the calendar. If you need to attend a meeting at a colleague's house, write the address and phone number right on the calendar. This will save you time if you need to contact that person; you won't have to search for the phone number or address the day of the meeting.

IT WORKED FOR HER

"Large wall calendar with color codes to show who is involved in the activity written next to each activity, write transportation needed and CIRCLE it: 'Dad drives,' 'Maryann picks up/car-pool,' or whatever."

Nancy E.

73. Add prompts to your calendar. Make a note of something that is happening in the future to remind yourself that it is coming up. For example, if you place an order by phone, make a note on the day by which the package should arrive. If the package is scheduled to be delivered within seven to ten days, count ten days forward on the calendar and make a note that the order should have been delivered by then. Also, make a note of when you placed the order, with whom, and the company's toll-free number. That way, if for any reason the item has not arrived, you can make a quick phone call to follow up about it without searching for the phone number or trying to remember whom you spoke with ten days ago. If the order has already arrived by the date on the calendar, simply cross it off.

74. Once you go through the trouble of writing all the information on the calendar, instead of rewriting the information if you'll need it again, simply make a note to refer back to the date with the information on it. So let's say you have an appointment scheduled with a new doctor and make a note of the office address and so on. If that appointment is rescheduled, instead of transcribing all that information, simply make a note on the new appointment day: "See Oct. 7 for the information."

75. To avoid spending time looking for papers relating to events you'll be attending (for example, tickets or party invitations), use a paper clip to attach them directly to your calendar.

76. If you tend to have too many pieces of paper to clip to a calendar, then consider buying a calendar with a pocket that can hold the papers.

77. Color-coding your calendar allows you to see things at a glance. Although it may seem like an added step that costs you time, in reality, as long as you have the supplies at hand, it saves you time and helps you feel more in control of your schedule. An added bonus is that family members can easily track their own events. Here's one of the easiest ways to color code: choose a different colored pen or highlighter for each member of the family, and use each family member's own color when writing in an item for that person. For example, write your son's soccer practice in blue or highlight it in blue, and write in the birthday party your daughter is attending with pink pen or highlight it in pink. Family events can be in another color or in Mom or Dad's color.

78. When looking over your calendar, think of what you plan to accomplish during the entire week instead of just that day. Days go by so quickly that you will be more successful if you plan out your weeks instead. Think horizontally, across the week, rather than just vertically about the hours in one day.

79. Stop wasting time flipping through your calendar looking for the current page. Place a sticky note or bookmark on the current page so you can easily turn to it, or tear off the corner of the page so you can reference that day's page easily.

80. Your calendar needs a home. Designate a single location and store it there. Once you go to all the trouble of writing things in your calendar, you need the security of knowing you'll be able to find it so you can reference it.

81. The calendar will only work if you look at it. Create a new routine of looking at your calendar throughout the day. If you have the space, leave the calendar open on your counter or desktop.

82. Write new items in the calendar directly instead of writing them on a piece of paper and then transcribing them into the calendar. Rewriting is a waste of time.

83. Shop online for a calendar. You may want to try these sites: www.daytimer.com, www.dayrunner.com, or www.calendars.com.

84. If you are using a paper version of a calendar and have recurring events, write them on a sticky note and move the note from month to month. If you want to remind yourself to pay the bills but you fear a little note on the calendar might be missed, you can write a reminder on a sticky note and move the note from month to month as you complete the task.

85. Keep your old calendars. Keeping the calendars from the past seven to ten years can save you lots of time. Not only will it serve as a record for tax purposes, but when you need the information from years gone by, you can locate it easily. Note: A great place to store the old calendars is with the corresponding tax year's paperwork.

86. If you have opted for an electronic calendar, you may find it helpful to store it in a case with a pen and paper for quick notes you need to write or as a back up in case the calendar is not functioning properly one day.

FIVE STEPS TO CHOOSE THE RIGHT PLANNER FOR YOU

Pick a planner. Remember there is no perfect planner, so just choose the one that comes closest to matching your style, and start to use it. Features to look for: portability, a calendar with enough space to write notes for each day, space to write a daily to-do list, blank note paper, a pen holder, and space to write in names and addresses. (Still not sure what planner is best for you? Visit www.jamienovak.com and take a quick quiz to find out.)

Pros and cons: paper versus electronic. Electronic organizers have a number of advantages. They are compact. You can program them to give you reminders, and recurring events only need to be entered once. They can organize lists at the click of a button. They can sort information and sync it with your other computers. If you learn to work with technology easily and you are willing to do the work to maintain the planner, like recharging the battery, then an electronic planner is right for you. If you need to see your whole week at a glance or don't have the energy to maintain an electronic version, then stick with pen and paper. (Even people with an electronic planner end up writing things down and then having to enter them, so no planner is completely paperless.)

You don't have to be overwhelmed by all the choices. Planners come in all shapes, sizes, and colors, as well as a variety of types. Make a list of the top three features you require in a planner and only look at those. For example, you may want a planner that doubles as a clutch purse or one that bends easily so you can cram it into an overstuffed bag.

In an effort to simplify, you may be tempted to try to keep two calendars. This actually makes things more difficult. You can forget where you wrote something, and inevitably you will double-book yourself. Plus, it actually wastes time, since you are then forced to check in two places instead of just one so you don't miss important events or appointments.

Give your planner a home. Just like everything you own, your planner needs a home and it needs to be put back immediately after every use. The home should be easy to remember and easy to access.

HOW TO GET THE MOST OUT OF YOUR PLANNER!

87. Fill your planner. Gather the items you commonly reference, and work in *small blocks of time* to enter information (like names, addresses, and phone numbers you use) into your new planner. Instead of using the alphabetical address section, consider using some of the pages for specific contact lists, like "play dates," "carpool," and "sports coaches." That way you can flip to the one page easily instead of looking through the entire book. Consider what vital information might be helpful to have in the planner, such as insurance policy numbers, computer passwords, equipment serial numbers, and birthdays and anniversaries, and enter this information in designated spaces.

88. Make your planner your new best friend and take it everywhere—shopping, to work, on the way to pick up the kids from school—absolutely everywhere. For it to do its job, it has to be with you. To remember to take your planner with you when you leave, place your keys on top of it.

89. Check your planner on a regular basis. Look over the next day's plans the night before and keep the planner open during the day to your daily to-do list.

90. Since remembering to check the calendar is usually half the battle, consider setting a timer or alarm as a reminder or posting sticky notes in obvious places to prompt you. Another helpful idea is to wrap this new habit around an existing habit; for example, check the planner at each meal or once before bedtime as you write out your to-do list for the next day. Two benefits to ending your day by looking at your calendar are: 1) it helps you to have a plan so you can hit the ground running in the morning, and 2) you can write out things that are on your mind so you can lie down in bed with a clear mind, making it easier to fall asleep.

91. Write in all your appointments, activities, and recurring tasks. You might find it helpful to use different colored pens for writing different types of things on your calendar (for example, red for appointments, blue for work activities, and green for family events). This allows you to recognize different types of events easily as your eye scans the page. For a very busy family, use a different color for each family member's activities.

5.

Managing Your To-Do List and Planning Ahead

92. When you have no structure, create it. In general, we tend to accomplish more when we have deadlines. Think about the day before you leave for vacation; somehow you manage to tick everything off your to-do list. Yet on days when you have the entire day to do stuff, you actually find yourself accomplishing less. To help keep you on track, you can create deadlines. For example, you might decide to join a friend for a midmorning grocery-shopping trip and write out the bills before you go. Now you have a deadline by which to finish the bills so that you can be ready to get the grocery shopping done. Without that structure in place, it could be very easy to bounce from project to project throughout the day, getting little or nothing truly accomplished, since you have the sense you can do anything at any time.

93. Schedule just 75 percent of your time; you need to allow for unexpected things. If you schedule all your time, you will undoubtedly fall behind and have no room to catch up.

94. Write it down. This simple task will immediately help you regain control over your time. The key is to write things in a single place, like a small spiral notebook that you can carry with you. (As with your planner, give your notebook a home so you'll always be able to find it.)

95. Stop making mental lists. Trying to remember everything is a big mistake; you can only remember so much, and often, forgetting means wasting time. For example, you might stop at the store to buy groceries but forget to buy an item that you really need, which means you'll have to make another trip to the store later. Plus, trying to keep track of everything in your head causes mental clutter and slows down your ability to do other tasks.

96. Control your daily to-do list. Your list should be comprised of five to ten tasks above and beyond your regular daily routines, like taxiing children and doing the dishes. Calling the bank to check on a charge that you don't recognize counts as one of the five to ten tasks. Grocery shopping, sorting through a pile of mail, and weeding the garden each count as one task. The goal is that by the end of the day you will have crossed off all the to-do items. Even if a limit of five to ten tasks seems too small, try to resist the urge to add more. Instead of a long list that is never accomplished, you'll have a short list that you can actually get through, after which you'll have the choice to stop for the day or start on the next day's list.

97. When you write items on your to-do list, group the similar items together—like with like. For instance, write the calls you have to make on one part of the page, all the errands you need to run on another part of the page, and so on.

98. Try a brain dump. Often we keep ideas and to-do items in our head and don't write them down. This wastes time. Take a few minutes and write down anything and everything you have been thinking about accomplishing. This list will most likely be long and somewhat overwhelming. This is *not* your to-do list! This is your master list. Once you see all that is on it, you can choose an item or two to work on when you have a moment. Then as one item is complete, you can move on to another master list item. (Keeping this list in your planner to add onto is helpful.)

99. Stop rewriting your list. If you have a list that needs to be rewritten at the end of the day, it means it is too long or you are writing the wrong things on the list; on most days you should be able to get those five to ten tasks accomplished. If you still have a list at the end of the day, look at what you are writing down. Are you limiting yourself to the top five to ten tasks, or are you writing a long list of things you *wish* you had time to accomplish? If so, the wish list items belong on their own piece of paper.

100. Set realistic goals. If you hope to organize your entire two-car garage in four hours, but currently can't even see the floor, it is doubtful you will reach your goal. Clearing both sides of the garage of all the piles of recycling might be a manageable goal instead. The great part about setting realistic goals is that you can reach them (and sometimes even surpass them), which puts you ahead. How many chances do we get to feel ahead in life?

101. Separating your to-do list into three sections—"urgent," "important," and "if I get to it"—is a simple way to get the top tasks accomplished without putting excess pressure on yourself.

102. Break up large tasks. When you have to do a large task that feels overwhelming, be sure to break it up into smaller, more doable tasks. For instance, if you need to swap your summer and winter wardrobes, *don't* plan to make the entire swap in one day. That task would feel too large to start, and you'd find yourself putting it off instead of getting started. Try breaking up the task into bite-sized pieces; for example, putting tank tops and shorts in one box; weeding your flip-flop collection and keeping only the good pairs; washing lightweight winter sweaters and taking winter jackets to the cleaners. Each one of these tasks is manageable, and you'll know specifically what to do.

103. Avoid wasting spare moments by making a task jar. Grab any jar you have sitting around, and keep it handy along with scraps of paper and a pen. Every time you think of a task that needs to be accomplished but that has no real deadline, like checking that all the pens in the pen cup work, write it on a sheet of paper. Pull a task from the jar when you have some time to kill (like while on hold during a phone call) or when you have just a few minutes before leaving the house. (But make sure you don't let the task make you late getting out the door!)

104. Test your to-do list for length by reciting it out loud. If, while describing the day ahead, you use the word "then" more than nine times you probably have more than ten items on your list you need to pare down. For example, "I'm going to drop the kids to school, *then* I'm going grocery shopping, *then* I've got the PTA meeting, *then* I'm going to the bank, and *then* the library, *then* I'm..." You get the picture; this is too many things on a single to-do list.

105. Give your to-do list items deadlines. If you don't set a date to have the task done by, it is less likely that the task will get done at all. Set final deadlines and smaller interim deadlines along the way to keep you on track. If you plan to have the family room repainted, knowing when you want to have the paint picked out and when you want the painter to start are all necessary tasks to complete before you can be sure how soon you need to start calling painters for estimates.

106. Do you prefer to work on the computer or do you need to share a to-do list with someone else? If so, then www.tadalist.com might be for you. Simply log on and register, then you can create lists and share them with others.

107. Instead of jotting to-do items on the backs of envelopes and sticky notes, grab your notebook and write it in the right place the first time. You won't waste time rewriting or looking for a lost scrap of paper. Plus, a single list takes a lot less time to read than notes on twenty crumpled up napkins, receipts, and scraps of paper.

108. Prioritize your list easily by looking at the consequences of putting off the task. For example, when trying to decide between paying the bills today or returning a library book, opt to pay the bills since a late fee assessed to your account could cost you upwards of $30, and a library fine will set you back about ten cents.

109. Often, you can do a task in less time than it takes to locate your to-do list and add the task. If the action will only take a couple minutes, consider just diving in and doing it, instead of adding it to your list.

110. There will be days and sometimes weeks where you need to deal with a specific project in addition to staying on top of all the regular everyday stuff. You might be planning a party, coordinating a house move, dealing with a crisis, or some other situation that takes time and attention. The trick is to balance all the balls in the air without dropping any. The easiest and least stressful way to do this is to make a plan. Pick specific times of the day to dedicate to the new project while keeping most of your day-to-day schedule intact. So if you were remodeling a room in your home, you might choose to deal with tasks relating to that project in the early afternoon every day. That way you know your day starts and ends the same as it always has, but you've left a space to pick out paint colors, return calls to contractors, review estimates, and so on. Without a plan, things might fall between the cracks.

6.

Stop Putting Yourself On Hold and Take Back Your Weekend

111. Although you could argue that addressing your needs should be last on the list since it takes time away from other things, the airlines teach us a valuable lesson in that regard: put on your own oxygen mask first. In the event of an emergency, you must place your own oxygen mask on first so that you are taken care of and better able to care for those around you. This principle is also true in day-to-day living. If you are not taken care of, there is no way you can take good care of anyone else.

112. Keep in mind that when you are not feeling 100 percent, everything takes longer and things that need your attention can pile up. If you don't take good care of yourself and you get sick, who is going to take care of the to-do list? If you rush around and are so distracted that you injure yourself, who can fill in for you? Taking care of you is a *necessity*, not a luxury.

113. It is okay to do nothing at all. Balance periods of intense doing with moments of doing nothing. It might feel like you are being lazy, but downtime is a necessity. If you do not allow your body the time to rest, you run the risk of doing too much, which can cause lots of problems.

114. I'm sure you've heard this one before, but I'll say it again: sleep, exercise, and eat well. Most days, this is easier said than done. Most of us hear those words and instantly form a picture of eating balanced meals, going to the gym, and sleeping eight or more hours every night. Since that is an unrealistic picture for most of us, we tend to give up before we even start. Instead of just giving up, try thinking outside the box. Where can you fit in a few extra minutes of moving per day? Can you park farther away in a parking lot so that you have to walk farther? Can you replace the bags of potato chips in your home with fresh fruit or crunchy vegetable slices? Can you pick one or two nights a week when, on a consistent basis, you'll hit the sheets earlier than normal no matter what, even if you have to leave things undone?

"If you take vitamins, get a pillbox with a week's worth listed. On Sunday (or one specific day a week), put all your vitamins out for one week's worth and fill your pillbox. This way you don't have to think about it all week, you just have to take your vitamins!"

Amy Stanley Greensburg, PA

115. You can't always just work on your to-do list. Without fun things in your life that you enjoy, you will quickly become bored. Identify things that bring you joy, and be sure to sprinkle a few into your week.

116. Taking a few quiet minutes for yourself in the morning gives you more energy, patience, and focus all day long. Don't pressure yourself to begin some drawn-out routine if that is not your style or if sitting quietly is a new routine for you altogether. You can read a few passages from an inspiring or spiritual book; you can listen to a relaxing song, write in a journal, or write a letter about your worries that you can then toss out. Even if you sit staring out the window or watching fish swim in a tank, you are doing a good thing. Just remember to set a timer so you don't go over your allotted time and then rush because you are running late—that would have the opposite effect of what you are trying to achieve.

117. Remember that you are the example for your children: they learn what they see. Showing them how to say "no," prioritize, care for themselves, and tackle a to-do list are life skills that they need. Otherwise, years from now, they will be reading this book and attending my workshops.

118. To help cut down on the time it takes you to apply makeup, try organizing your makeup by type. If there are specific products you use for nighttime only, place those in one bag. That way you won't have to rifle through everything to find your anytime lip gloss. Keep a separate bag for those days when you just want to apply your gloss and mascara. If you store your makeup directly in the makeup bag, then once you apply it you can grab the bag, toss it in your purse, and be out the door.

119. Keep your favorites on hand. If you have an absolute favorite piece of makeup, maybe a lipstick that goes with everything that you wear all the time, then splurge and get a second one. That way you can keep one at home and one in your bag. You might also opt for a complete second set of all your standby pieces, so you can leave one set in your bag, your desk drawer at work, or somewhere else, and leave the originals at home.

120. To save even more time, skip the fancy makeup bag and opt for a food storage bag instead. Not only can you see through it clearly, you can toss it when it gets gunked up.

121. Have a plan B in the event you experience a bad hair day. Without a plan for how to wear your hair if your original style does not turn out as you wanted it to, you will end up wasting valuable time trying to tame your 'do. This might mean keeping a headband, cute hair clips, or even a hat, on hand.

122. Whenever you can, prep your hair in advance. If you flat iron your curls, do it in the evening, or if you put in curlers, do it early and let them set as you get ready. Ionic blow-dryers have been reported to cut drying time in half, if you have to blow dry at all; sometimes you can get away with air drying, or at least air drying most of the way and touching up with a dryer. Whenever you can, allow your hair to go more natural; the more natural the style, the less work and time it takes.

123. Choose multitasking products whenever possible to remove extra steps in your routines. Some examples are makeup products that can be used on your cheeks and eyelids, shampoos with conditioners in them, facial moisturizers with tinting, body creams with sunblock, etc.

124. Do you have trouble leaving the thoughts of the day behind and relaxing for the evening? Creating a simple routine that you follow daily can help signal your body to start to shut out the day and focus on being quiet. Playing relaxing music, filling the air with calming scents such as lavender, or sitting quietly and reviewing the day in your mind can all help.

125. Sometimes it can be uncomfortable for things around us to become quiet. Without any distractions, we are forced to sit alone and think. That may not always be comforting, especially when the to-dos start to flood our minds. Keep a pad and pen or voice recorder at your bedside, and when you think of something, jot it down; once it is out of your mind, you can stop thinking about it and know that you will be able to deal with it later. (If you tend to wake up during the night and these thoughts come to you, keep a flashlight near the bed so you can write notes without turning on a bright light.)

126. Go list-less and time-less one day a week. This is very important. If you always feel like you are on a schedule, then you might start to resent it. To avoid boredom, choose one day of the week where you do not have a regimented schedule. Opt not to wear a watch on that day and avoid creating a to-do list. If you want to, you can jot a few things on a sticky note that would be nice to get done if you choose to.

127. You do not have to spend tremendous amounts of time to pamper yourself. There are many quick exercises that can calm you down and release stress. Here's one routine to try: sit with your eyes closed and take three deep breaths—in through your nose and out through your mouth; scrunch your shoulders up towards your ears and hold for a count of five, then release; repeat a few times and your muscles will feel less tense. Look up and focus on one corner of the room at a time for ten seconds per corner. When you look back down, your eyes will feel better, and you'll be more relaxed.

128. Rethink how you view playtime. Too often we criticize ourselves for not getting more of the "right" things done. However, during our time "off" we are either recharging our energy, spending time with people we care about, being alone, or doing something that we wouldn't initially classify as work but that actually is. Stop thinking of downtime as an unproductive waste of time. Instead, choose to classify downtime as important business.

IT WORKED FOR HER

"When my toddler is taking a bath, I soak my feet in the tub with him for ten minutes. Then I use a foot scrub, followed by a nice lotion. I have soft, smooth feet without taking any extra time!"

Ruth Ann Lewis Avon, NY

129. Tired of being busy all week and then having to spend your weekends running errands and doing even more household chores? Here's the quick fix: grab your calendar and block off two weekend days per month. Those days will be your free weekend days, and it is important that you refrain from committing to doing *anything* on those days. Then, be smarter about using your weekdays. Can you run errands on your lunch hour or once the children are in bed? Can you shop online, limiting the number of trips you need to make to the store? Since there will always be more to do, if you don't take action to take back your weekends, they will all slip through your fingers.

130. Keep in mind that almost everything takes longer on the weekends since more people are out and about. Roads have more traffic, parking lots are fuller, lines are longer, shelves are less stocked, and so on. It usually makes sense to get whatever you can do done during the week.

HAVE MORE TIME TODAY!

1. Use your calendar or planner in more effective ways.
2. Write out a daily to-do list as your game plan for the day.
3. Prepare at night for the next day.

TRY THIS:

Find three ways to maximize your calendar. Give your calendar a home today, and from now on, always put it back when you are done with it, so you can find it again.

REPEAT AFTER ME:

"I feel great about all I accomplished today!"

Part Three:

What Exactly Do You Do All Day?

Do you ever find yourself with big plans of what you'll accomplish during the day, but then by the end of the day realize you haven't done the things on your list? You've been busy all day long but you can't figure out where the time went or what you've been doing? That can happen to the best of us. Most likely you suffer from the zigzag syndrome. The zigzag syndrome is common and easily identifiable: you'll find yourself setting off to do something with the very best of intentions, but then something else catches your eye and you are off doing that. For example, you go to make your bed and find a glass of water on your nightstand, so you run it down to the dishwasher and see the washer is full, so you go to turn it on but you are out of soap, so you go to the basement to grab a new box of detergent and while you are in the basement you start folding the last load of clothes from the dryer before they wrinkle. It's now noon, your bed never got made, and you're tired! Sound familiar? If you work from home, you can feel even more like a ping-pong ball! Here are some of the best remedies for combating the zigzag syndrome.

7.

Chores

131. Creating a simple schedule for your chores is a good way to manage them and to avoid feeling like you are doing those same chores each and every day. Pull out your calendar and choose specific days of the week to do certain chores. You might want to grocery shop on Thursday evenings after the children go to bed and your spouse can watch them. That way the store shelves are stocked, the lines are short, the parking is easy, and you can run in and out without children in tow. You might even toss in loads of laundry on Monday and Wednesday evenings before bed so they are dry by breakfast and you can fold everything once the children are out the door to school. Having a schedule that works for you keeps you on track and makes your life easier. Create your own schedule based on your lifestyle; try it out for a week, and then make any necessary adjustments.

132. Avoid zigzagging through the house as you attempt to accomplish chores. It can be so easy to bounce from one chore to another; you might be changing the sheets on the bed and notice the corner of the rug could use a quick vacuum, so you pull out the vacuum and then you go to the kitchen to empty the canister and, before you know it, the linens are still not changed. Stick to your game plan and see the first task through, start to finish. If you notice something along the way that needs your attention, simply jot it down and get to it later. This includes delivering items to other rooms in the house: make one pile and distribute all the items once your initial task is complete.

133. Swap chores when you notice you lack the motivation for the job. We can only scrub showers so many years before we start to feel a little less enthused about the job. Rotate the jobs, even for a week or two, so you can get a reprieve while finding a new "challenge" in a chore, like tying up newspapers for recycling.

134. Delegate as many chores as you can. Take a moment to create a list of all the chores that need to be accomplished in any given month. Then, next to each, write the initials of the person who is currently in charge of getting it done. Review the list to see which of the chores can be delegated to someone else in the household. Keep in mind that although someone else may not complete the chore exactly how you would, his or her way still gets it done and frees up your time. Plus, more importantly, this teaches others how things are done so they can become self-sufficient.

135. Hire out the chore whenever you can. Sometimes it just does not make sense for you to do the chore when there is someone out there who has made a profession of it and has the skills, the supplies, and the enthusiasm to complete the job. When you weigh your time against a professional's fee to complete the job, it might turn out to be one of the best investments you've ever made. If your budget doesn't currently have the wiggle room to fit this in, then look at what you can cut out. Unused gym memberships, subscriptions to magazines you don't read, and takeout meals all add up; that money could be redirected towards freeing you from an unpleasant chore.

136. If it is not within your budget to hire out chores, consider hiring someone as a special treat either around the holidays, for your birthday, or simply when you've set aside enough money. A gift certificate for housecleaning, errand running, or lawn care makes a wonderful gift for someone to give you or for you to give to someone who already has everything.

137. Whenever it makes sense, combine chores. Combining them is different from bouncing from one task to another. When you combine chores, you'll accomplish two related tasks simultaneously—like washing your car and the dog at the same time since you'll need to have the garden hose out for both.

138. Pick one time a month to tackle minor home repairs. Instead of pulling out the hammer, screwdriver, and can of oil multiple times, do it only once. Keep a short list hanging inside the pantry door and every time you think of a repair, jot it down, then pull out all the supplies and complete them at one time.

139. Tackle minor home repairs before they become large, time-consuming, budget-busting repairs. What is a small leak now can quickly turn into damaged wallboards, rusted pipes, and other water damage.

140. Make chores fun! Put on some music, have a friend pop by to chat as you work, or make a game out of the chore by setting a timer and challenging yourself to see what you can accomplish before the timer buzzes.

8.
Laundry

141. Spend less time matching socks! Keep socks paired together through the laundry with the Sock Pro or Sock Cop. These products keep a matched pair of socks together throughout the washing and drying process.

142. If you prefer not to use a clip like the Sock Cop or Sock Pro, then you can simply use a lingerie bag to contain and wash all the socks for one family member in his or her own bag—no more missing socks; and yes, the socks will be clean. And if you've ever wondered where the missing socks are going, don't look for them in the dryer; they are usually lost in the washer when they float over the edge of the drum and sink down by the motor.

143. Save time putting away everyone else's laundry by leaving the completed laundry for that family member on his or her bed when age appropriate (which may be earlier than you think), and make it a new family rule that they are to put all the laundry away before bedtime.

144. Designate a drop-off area for dirty laundry and a pick-up area for clean laundry. No more running all over the house to collect dirty laundry. Instead, make it a new family rule that any items left in the designated spot on laundry day will be washed. Anything not in the spot will have to wait until the next wash cycle.

145. Make a simple schedule for yourself so you know when you wash the family bath towels and rugs, the bed sheets, the kitchen towels, and so on. If you have a routine for the larger, bulkier items, you'll stop running extra loads because you forgot to toss them in.

146. Save even more time by taking comforters, sleeping bags, and other oversize items to the laundromat for them to wash and fold or for you to do there. The industrial strength machines wash and dry faster; plus, you don't use your electricity and water, and you save the motor on your machines.

147. Set the laundry area up in such a way that you have everything you need within reach. If you are short on space near the washer and dryer, then create space; even a folding table or a computer armoire with a slide-out shelf meant to hold the keyboard can do the job.

148. Cut ironing time in half by placing a sheet of aluminum foil under the garment (shiny side up); the heat will reflect and two sides will be done simultaneously.

149. Consider multitasking when ironing or folding. No one says you have to do those tasks in the laundry room. You can help children with homework, watch a movie, or talk on the phone using a headset while doing the folding.

150. Stop living out of laundry baskets. Once the wash is clean and folded, it is much quicker to take a few minutes to put it away than to live out of the basket. Clothes get unfolded very quickly, and then it is unclear what is still clean; items that are not even dirty often get tossed into the dirty laundry pile.

151. Have clear guidelines about what constitutes an item that is ready to be laundered. Stop wasting time pulling socks right side out and checking pants pockets. Instead, make it a new household rule that these things need to be done before the items hit the dirty laundry pile. (Also make it clear that just because something is wrinkled doesn't mean it automatically gets tossed in the dirty laundry pile; running the iron over it, hanging it on a hanger and leaving it in the bathroom while you take a hot shower, or tossing it in the dryer on the air cycle can be much faster.)

152. Make room in the dresser and closet to put away clothing. Unused off-season clothing often takes up valuable space in dresser drawers and in the closet, which makes it more time-consuming to put away clothing that is used. Remove the articles of clothing that have not been used in a season. You can store them elsewhere or opt to donate them.

153. Save time by using the right product to fight a stain. Stop wasting time trying different methods and risking ruining the item for good. (Refer to the stain treatment chart in the resource section of the book. You might even make a copy or print one off my website, www.jamienovak.com, and hang it where you store your stain-treating solutions.)

154. Toss in a load of laundry before you go to bed to let it wash overnight while you sleep; then dry it in the morning.

155. Cut laundry time by presorting items into baskets labeled "towels," "jeans," "darks," "lights," "dry-clean only," and so on. A triple laundry sorter can be very helpful for this task; each bag holds two loads of laundry, and you can sort directly into the bags. No more piling all the laundry together and then resorting. (Note: You are not the only one who is capable of sorting clothing. By showing others in the house how to do it, you are helping them to learn the process so they can repeat it when you are not there to do it for them.)

156. Before you do a load of wash, wipe off the front and sides of the washer and dryer with a damp cloth, then toss the cloth in with the laundry. This will keep dust and lint from collecting on the machines.

157. Organize bed sheets into sets using one of the pillowcases from each set as its container. Place the folded flat sheets, fitted sheets, and other pillowcases into one of the pillowcases from the set; that way you can save time by grabbing a complete set right away instead of searching for the matching pieces.

158. Store bedding where you use it. Keep the set for the mattress in the room either on a shelf in a closet, in a dresser drawer, or between the mattress and box spring. Store guest bedding somewhere other than your family's linen closet. Try an ottoman or bench in the guest room that lifts up for storage.

159. Attach a stain stick to the laundry hamper; you can easily pretreat stains as you put clothes inside the hamper.

160. Put everything that can't be machine-dried into a large mesh sweater bag before you wash it so that you can easily identify the pieces when the wash cycle is done and not mistakenly toss them into the dryer.

161. Make it a policy not to wash any-thing that is in need of mending. If you have a skirt that needs a new button, mend it before you wash it. This saves you lots of time in the long run since you won't be tempted to place the item back into your closet and then grab it one day, only to remember that it still needs a button, forcing yourself to spend precious time that morning rethinking your wardrobe choice.

IT WORKED FOR HER

"We keep the dry cleaning receipt in the bottom of our dry cleaning bag; it will always be there when we drop off our dry cleaning. I empty out the bag, give the lady my receipt, and put the new receipt right into the now empty bag. Then we fill up the bag for the week with the receipt safely at the bottom. No more spending time searching for lost receipts or forgetting to pick up the dry cleaning."

Catherine G. Fanwood, NJ

162. Try a home-based dry cleaning kit; many work just as well or better than dragging the clothes to the dry cleaners. This saves you the time of running to and from the dry cleaners and paying the high prices. Plus, you won't be stuck with all those plastic dry cleaning bags and wire hangers.

163. Stop wasting time trying to untangle wire nests of hangers from the dry cleaners. Instead, use a hanger organizer (from any organizing store) to keep them orderly, and then you can either reuse them or return them to the dry cleaner.

164. You can avoid ironing many articles of clothing by drying them properly. Hang drying or lying clothes flat to dry really does help. If you are short on drying rack space, try installing a second bath towel rod or a pullout drying rack that can be closed up when not in use. (If ironing is not your favorite task, try to buy only items that do not require ironing. Eventually you will have all ironless clothes in your wardrobe.)

165. Save time hanging blouses on hangers by buttoning the top-collar button before you put the blouses in the wash. When they come out, you can slip them onto a hanger without them falling off.

166. If you do not want to spend money on costly non-slip hangers, then create your own. By adding non-skid pads meant for the soles of shoes or the bathtub onto the edges of hangers, you can create your own non-slip hangers at a fraction of the cost; plus, you spend less time picking up clothing that has slipped off the hangers.

167. To avoid having to iron an entire load of laundry left in the dryer too long, simply toss in a damp towel and dry the load again on a warm—not hot—setting.

IT WORKED FOR HER

"Whenever I have clothes that need to be ironed, especially golf shirts or slacks, I keep them in a spare closet "inside out" so I can quickly identify my ironing. I also accumulate it all for a rainy day."

Eloise, Mountainside, NJ

168. Stop wasting time trying to read the faded tags inside the articles of clothing for the washing instructions. Instead, hang up a bulletin board where you can post the washing instructions. On the board you can also place a stain chart, needles with thread, a few extra buttons, and anything else you find yourself reaching for when dealing with laundry.

169. Instead of delivering items found in the pockets of the clothing back to their owners, place all the lost-and-found in a single box; if someone is missing something, he or she can check the lost-and-found box for it.

170. If possible, build a laundry chute that leads directly into the laundry room or, better yet, put your laundry room on the same level as the bedrooms.

9.

Working and Working from Home

171. By starting your day with a power hour, you will get more done than you ever have before. When you first sit down to work, *do not* open your email, check your voice mail, or answer the phone; instead focus solely on one project. You might choose to get two or three small things done that have been piling up; you might file or do some other project that has been continuously pushed to the side as a low priority; or you might work on a small piece of a much bigger project so that you can get it done little by little and not have to rush at the last minute. Set a timer for your power hour or power half hour (if that's all the time you've got, some is still better than none), and when the timer rings, start your day.

172. Do like tasks together; instead of getting up from your desk multiple times throughout the day to fax something, make it a routine to fax once or twice a day and combine it with another task that requires getting up and walking in that general direction. So you might get up for a cup of coffee on your way to the meeting and fax something along the way.

173. If the task will take some time and you can leave it running by itself, do so and come back for it later. You may need to copy a one-hundred-page report: you could stand and watch it copy, or you could let it run and go do another task in the meantime. You might be surprised what else you can accomplish while waiting for something else to process.

174. Save even more time by setting up your email system to automatically respond to incoming emails with an email letting the sender know that his or her email has been received and that you check emails at a certain time of the day. You can also list a few colleagues and their contact information, suggesting that for immediate attention, they contact the person best suited to answer their questions.

175. You will work faster and make fewer mistakes when your eyes are fresh and your mind has had a short break. Set a timer to remind you every twenty to thirty minutes to turn away from the computer screen, stretch, have a sip of water, and then get back to work before you lose your train of thought. This also means you *must* take your lunch break. Contrary to popular belief, working through lunch to get something done is not helpful; when you are tired and stressed, you tend to make more mistakes and work more slowly. You would, in fact, be better off stepping away from your desk and eating something, even going outside for a breath of fresh air. When you return to your desk, you will be refreshed and ready to tackle the project more effectively.

176. Program your outgoing voice mail message with the answers to callers' most frequently asked questions—things like your fax number, email address, or the name of the person to call if they need immediate assistance. Ideally, the caller's question will be answered and he or she will not leave a message, which means you'll have fewer phone calls to return.

177. Having routines allows you to more easily schedule your day, since you know what to expect most of the time, saving you time and effort. Leave time in between routines and scheduled activities for emergencies, as well as overflow if a project runs long. Try adding routines to your week; write a short list of five to ten tasks that need to be accomplished on a weekly basis. Then assign one or two per day, try your new routine for a week, and make adjustments as necessary.

178. Delegate whenever possible. For the next week, as you complete a task, think about whether or not you are the best person to do it in the future. If not, find someone who can share the task with you or take it over.

179. When you are given an assignment, ask what the deadline is. Even if you are told it's a "rush," that can mean different things to different people. Clarify when results are needed, and prioritize accordingly.

180. Give and get clear instructions. When you or someone else is unclear about how to carry out the task, it takes longer and there is more probability it will be done incorrectly. (Always ask when you are unclear about what you are expected to do; this saves you the time and hassle of redoing it.)

181. Whenever you can, complete just part of a job and turn it in for approval. Then, when you are sure you are on the right track, complete the job. No sense doing the entire job and turning it in only to find out it is not correct and you have to redo it. An added bonus to this trick is that sometimes the person will finish it up himself or herself, freeing up your time! (If you are the one giving the instructions, ask the person to show you what they have done before they finish it so you can check the progress and be sure they are on the right track.)

182. Set a timer at your desk for blocks of time during which you will focus on a particular task without answering the phone or jumping to work on another project. I suggest working in eighteen minute blocks of time. This is enough time to see progress but not so much time that you'll continue putting off getting started.

183. Keep in mind that a task will expand to fit the amount of time allotted. If you set aside two hours to write a report, you can do it in the allotted time. But if you set aside four hours for that same report, it will take that much longer. Challenge yourself to get things done in a shorter period of time and plan accordingly.

184. Be sure to block out time in your calendar to follow up and to catch up. Without an actual dedicated block of time to do these things, they will either be left undone or they will be crammed into your day, meaning that everything else will get pushed back and you will end up running late or leaving something else undone.

185. Your pile of items "to be read" will not be accomplished in your spare time. You must schedule time in your week or month to read. If you still find yourself short on time, try an executive summary service that offers the highlights from many of the most popular books on sale today; check out www.summary.com.

186. Filing is another task that is never completed in your spare time. If you find a pile of to-be-filed papers building, consider moving your files around to make it easier to keep them updated. You will have more success filing when you can easily reach the files without getting up from your chair. It's not about being lazy; it's just that when you are busy, you need a task to be easy so it won't disrupt your workflow or take more time than necessary. If a rolling file cart will work for you, try that; if a small filing credenza next to your desk makes sense, then do that. But stop piling!

187. Avoid wasting time preparing for and going to an appointment, only to find out it was cancelled. Take a quick moment to confirm your appointments before you make the trip.

188. Save lots of time in the morning by spending five to ten minutes at the end of each day wrapping up and preparing for the next day. Put away things you used during the day, including files. Then pull out what you'll need for the next day, and leave that on your chair or front and center on your desk.

189. Use your prime time. There are specific times of the day when we tend to be at our peak and others when we lull, like an hour after lunch. Do the most mentally taxing activity that requires focus and precision at the times when you are at your best, leaving rote tasks, like filing, to do when you are less energetic.

190. Do not place an extra chair by your desk; this will deter people from dropping by your office to chat and overstaying their welcome. Additionally, a chair by your desk can easily become a catchall for clutter, which you'll then have to spend time sorting through and putting away.

191. Try making a people page in your spiral notebook. On a fresh sheet of paper, jot down everyone you need to meet with or talk to, and next to his or her name write what you need to discuss. The next time you talk with a person, you will have all the issues to discuss on hand. This will save you time since you will be less likely to forget something and have to make another time to talk with him or her. Also, you'll get the points down on paper and out of your mind. (Saving up your questions to ask at one time and asking others to do the same for you means everyone is interrupted less.)

192. Whenever possible, opt for conference calls in lieu of an in-person meeting.

193. When asked to take on another task, remind the person who's asking what you are already working on and ask for clear priorities of what should be done first. Always ask, "When do you need this by?" so you are both clear on the deadline. And feel free to try to negotiate the deadline; often it is not set in stone.

194. Having an open-door policy does not mean that your door has to actually be open every minute of the day. Instead, post a list of times when coworkers are welcome to come to you for advice; when you need time alone, shut your door.

195. When you are in the middle of a project that requires your full attention, post a sign that reads, "Please don't disturb. Genius at work" to alert people of the fact that you do not wish to be interrupted. You can also post a sign with a time when you'd prefer for them to come back. Lastly, if your project is portable, take all the pieces and work somewhere away from your desk, like a conference room or an empty office.

196. Face your desk away from the door if you can to avoid looking up as people pass. When you catch someone's eye as he or she walks by, the person is more likely to stop and chat.

197. If you have the option, try having your visitors screened. Give clear instructions to the person who is screening about who should be allowed to drop in, and be sure you have an understanding about what situations demand that the rules be broken and the person allowed to stop in.

198. When people ask for your time, take control of the situation and go to see them. That way you can guide the conversation and leave when you need to. You should also ask how much of your time they anticipate needing; then you can hold them to that number and if they run over, say that you have to go but you can come back later. You might also ask if there is anything you can prepare, so you can have it ready when you meet.

199. Whenever someone comes into your office, stand up to talk with him or her. Once people sit down, the conversation automatically gets longer. Stand up, and if the person is known for being on the chatty side, offer to walk and talk with him or her. You can get a lot accomplished on your way to get a cup of coffee or on your way to lunch. And it is generally understood that the conversation is over when you reach the destination.

HAVE MORE TIME TODAY!

1. Create a schedule of chores, so you don't end up trying to do everything every day.
2. Take one step out of the laundry process by using a triple sorter.
3. Be sure to take real breaks during the day so you can recharge and gear up for the next task.

TRY THIS:

Choose one new household rule and put it in place starting today. You might try, "In our house we put clothes in the hamper right side out," or "In our house we clip our socks together before we put them in the wash," or "In our house we empty our pockets *before* we put our clothes into the hamper."

REPEAT AFTER ME:

"I'm focused on the task at hand, seeing it through from start to finish."

Part Four:

Meals and More

It's six o'clock and your child asks the dreaded question, "What's for dinner?" You wish you knew the answer. Unfortunately, it's like a pop quiz since you forgot to take anything out of the freezer. You opt to order out again, wondering how everyone else does it. You are pretty sure there are people out there who are cooking meals that are ready at dinnertime and that their families like, but you wonder how they do it. I've decoded the mystery for you, and trust me, it's not as difficult as you think.

10.
Meal Planning
and Pantry

200. Planning your meals will save you countless hours and lots of stress. But preparing a meal plan is not as complicated as you might think; in fact, you already have one! What you have been cooking is your meal plan; the difference is that now you need to write it down. Simply grab your calendar and go back a week or two, writing in any of the meals you remember making that everyone ate. Then for the next week or so, track the meals you make. At the end of four weeks you have a month's meal plan.

201. Take that month's worth of meals and consider grouping all of a like kind of meal on a day of the week for a themed meal plan. For example, Monday can be pasta night; Tuesday, Mexican or tacos; Wednesday, mac and cheese; Thursday, chicken; and so on. This can help you save time thinking about what to make since you already know what the main ingredient or theme is for that day. (For even more ideas on meal planning including a step-by-step system, visit www.jamienovak.com.)

202. You can take the themed meal idea even further and save yourself more time by putting meals that use similar ingredients on back-to-back days. Like a spaghetti dish with ground beef on day one, then tacos with ground beef the next day so you can cook all the meat on day one and save half for day two.

203. Once you have your meal plan written out for the month, you can save time shopping by noting the two types of ingredients you need to make each meal. List the non-perishable items that you can buy in one large shopping trip at the start of the month. Separately list the perishable items you'll need to buy weekly to make the meals for that week. Note: Save even more time by having a bulk order delivered once a month by the grocery store or other online retailer like www.amazon.com.

204. Not sure who will like dinner and who might boycott it the next time you make it? Ask everyone to rate the meal from one to five stars; then jot the rating next to the meal on your calendar. Eventually you can replace all the lower-rated meals with five-star meals.

205. Share the task. You don't have to be the only one spending time thinking of meals. Ask each family member to offer two or three ideas of meals he or she would eat without a fuss.

206. Don't waste time by overcomplicating the meal planning system. A simple calendar with the meals listed or index cards with the recipe on front and the shopping list on the back will work just fine.

207. For your meal plan to work, you will need to build in a little room for flexibility. There will be days when the meal cannot be made as planned.

IT WORKED FOR HER

"To help make meal planning easier in my house, I have a laminated page of our most popular dinners. Every week I sit down and make a menu for a week or week and a half—keeping in mind all activities, so when I need something quick I am prepared. The day I go grocery shopping I do as much prep work as I can for upcoming meals. Like cutting chicken and then freezing (if needed), washing lettuce for salad, etc."

Dawn

208. Leave yourself a note to remind yourself to take frozen meat or ingredients out of the freezer. Still can't remember? Place your car keys in the freezer and you'll have to remember before you can leave the house for the day. (It will only take about twenty-one days to create a new habit, so you won't have to freeze your keys forever.)

209. Another big timesaver is prepping dinner while making lunch. Say you need chopped vegetables for dinner: cut the dinner vegetables at lunchtime, so they'll be ready to go for that evening, and use some of the vegetables to make a salad for lunch.

210. Stop wasting time searching for the recipe you clipped and now can't find. Instead, take a three-ring binder, fill it with clear plastic sheet protectors, and slide your recipe clippings into the plastic protectors for safekeeping and easy reference.

211. Keep your pantry stocked. The more items you have on hand, the less time you have to spend stopping at the store to pick up missing items. Save time by adding tiered shelves to your cabinets and pantry. With everything visible, you'll spend less time searching through the cabinets and pantry.

212. Baskets, wire or clearly labeled wicker, can make an attractive option in your pantry; you can toss in grab-and-go foods like bags of chips, packs of gum, or nutritional bars. It saves time when you can grab the food and go without struggling with a lid or packaging. If you like wicker baskets but have a difficult time finding attractive labeling options, try using a tag meant for scrapbooking. Print the name on the tag, then attach it with a little ribbon. Another double-duty option is to buy material liners for the basket and have a tailor embroider the name on the part of the liner that folds over the outside of the basket.

213. Try spending one day cooking multiple meals that store well; then use them throughout the week. Lasagnas, stews, and some casseroles all keep well. Clearly label the dishes before freezing and consider listing the cooking instructions. If you'll use some as lunches, store them in individual portion sizes.

214. Want some company as you cook? Invite friends and family over to cook with you. Each of you can cook a different meal in extra-large portions and split the complete dishes. If you each prefer to cook at different times or the kitchen is too small to accommodate everyone, cook in your own homes and deliver the meals to each person or meet in a central location to give the meals to one another. Consider giving the container with your name to the person in advance so he or she can fill it and you won't have to worry about giving back the container the food came in.

215. Stop wasting time looking for your take-out menus. Grab a three-ring binder and fill it with a handful of clear plastic three-hole punched sheet protectors. Slip one menu into each page protector. Another option is to place all the menus into a single slash pocket folder.

216. Place a second set of take-out menus in the car for easy reference on those days when you need the information and you are not home. Also, store the phone numbers for your favorite restaurants in your cell phone with "R" in front of each entry so you can go directly to the restaurants on the list.

217. Instead of going to a restaurant and placing your order for take-out when you arrive, try calling the order in. You can read the restaurant's menu online or keep a three-ring binder of the printed menus for your favorite restaurants. (Don't three-hole punch the menus; instead, slide them into clear plastic sheet protectors.) When you call ahead, the food will be ready when you arrive, and you'll spend much less time waiting in line.

218. When going to a new restaurant, you can save time by viewing the restaurant's menu online before you go. You won't have to decide right then what you want to order, but you'll get more familiar with the menu, since often menus are a few pages long and you can spend a lot of time trying to read small print in a dark restaurant.

219. Make a grab-and-go section in your kitchen. Designate one drawer or basket in the kitchen for snack bars and small bags of snacks. You can easily make your own snack-size bags by filling ziplock bags from bulk containers of snacks.

220. One of the biggest timesavers, especially when just starting out with the meal planning system, is to set a timer to go off when you need to start dinner. Some days you're so busy that by the time you look at the clock, it is already too late to start cooking the meal. Setting the timer to remind you to start preparing dinner can be a huge timesaver.

221. When you are entertaining and want to serve a meal where the main dish and side dishes are all ready at the same time, follow this time management tip: make a timeline. Take a letter-size piece of paper and at the bottom write the time that you plan to serve the meal. Then work backwards, adding in all the other items and the preparation for them. For example, for a turkey dinner with two side dishes and hot rolls to be served at 6:00 p.m., you would work backwards to calculate when the turkey needs to be put in the oven. If it will take five hours to cook, it needs to go into a 350-degree oven at 1:00 p.m., which means you need to preheat the oven at 12:45 p.m. Write "12:45 preheat oven to 350" near the top of the paper, since that is one of the first things you'll need to do. Then fill in the timeline with the time to put the rolls on a cookie sheet and bake them and the time to create the two side dishes. You can even add in the time to set the table, heat the gravy, toss the salad, and so on. (Posting your timeline on the front of your refrigerator or somewhere else you can easily reference it is key. Also, use a timer to keep you on track, setting it at intervals to remind you to begin the next task; a portable timer is preferable since you can carry it with you when you leave the kitchen.)

11.

Grocery Shopping

222. Cut down on all of your trips to the store by shopping over the Internet. Most grocery stores offer a delivery service for a small fee; often that fee is offset by special offers or the fact that you won't be wasting money picking up impulse items since you will not be in the store. Even if you prefer to pick out perishable items yourself, you can opt to have just the big items delivered. Imagine the time you'll save not having to shop for and carry in bags and bags of bottled water, cat litter, and paper towels. (Many grocery stores offer a shop and pick-up service where they shop for you and all you have to do is pick up the bags at a specified time. This is a great option if you are already out running errands anyway.)

223. Market Day is a nationally run organization that gives a percentage of the grocery shopping sales back to the school system. Here's how it works: you place your order and then pick up the food when you pick up your child from school. Note: You can use the service even if you do not have children in the school.

224. Stop by customer service at your local grocery store and ask for an in-store aisle guide; use it to organize your shopping list. (Sometimes the guides are available online as well.)

IT WORKED FOR HER

"This takes a little planning but saves oodles of time once you get this system arranged. It's a store specific grocery list. Make a list of items aisle-by-aisle in your favorite grocery store. Next to each item put an underline mark '_' so that you can check it when you run out of something or are making your list, e.g., 'Aisle 3, Cereal_.' Make numerous copies to have on hand or readily available on the computer to print out. Next, organize your coupon envelope according to aisle. When shopping, it's a breeze to zip down each aisle with the list and coupons corresponding to the aisle."

Carol

225. Write out or type up a master shopping list including food, dry goods, cleaning supplies, toiletries, paper products, and so on; then make fifty-two copies of it. Start a new sheet each week, simply checking off what you need to buy.

226. Organize your master shopping list by the arrangement of aisles in your favorite grocery store. Having the items listed in order will save you a tremendous amount of time in not backtracking through the store.

227. Post a master shopping list on your refrigerator or on the inside of your cabinet door. When an item runs low, mark it on your list. Share this new routine with everyone in your family. You might even Velcro a pen or highlighter near the list; simply put a small square of self-adhesive Velcro on the pen or highlighter and another on the door next to the list. Another "greener" option is to laminate the master list and use dry erase markers on it, which you can then wipe off to reuse the list week after week.

228. Have everyone who lives in the house agree on what constitutes "almost empty," so you can replenish ahead of time and will not have to run out in the middle of cooking.

229. Mark your list with the letter "C" next to items that you have coupons for so you know when to check for sizes and brands. (It may save you even more time to write the size and brand right on your list.)

230. Read the store's circular before going to the store. That way you can zip through the store without getting caught up reading the in-store sale signage.

231. Stop wasting time clipping coupons you never use. Allow yourself to forgo the coupon clipping for a period of time until you get your new meal planning system in place. Then you can add the coupons back in.

232. Get to know where your store tends to stack special sale items; that way you won't waste time looking on the shelf if they are normally stacked at the end of an aisle.

233. Don't get caught in the store without your coupons. Clipping coupons and then not using them is a waste of time and money. Make it a habit to paper clip the coupons for the week directly to the shopping list. (If you prefer envelopes, then tuck the coupons in an envelope, and write your list on the outside of the envelope. It is possible to print your master list directly on the outside of the envelope using your computer.)

234. Whenever possible, shop *without* little children but *with* a partner. Your spouse, family member, or friend can speed up the shopping process. As one grabs items from one aisle, the other can go to the next section. You truly will be done in half the time, and having someone with you makes it more fun and easier to carry in the bags. Shopping with someone can allow you to socialize as you shop, which is a great way to multitask.

235. Avoid crowds by shopping late at night or early in the morning just after the store opens. Early Sunday morning is a particularly good time—the shelves are freshly stocked, the parking lot is less full, lines are shorter, and the entire trip is more enjoyable.

236. Don't allow yourself to become side-tracked by browsing items not on your list, and don't get sucked into the magazine and book sections. These diversions can eat up valuable time. Unless you have spare time, steer clear!

237. Bag your own groceries, so you can pack things together in the way they are stored in your home. This will save you time unpacking. (If you have frozen items but are not planning on going directly home, you can keep them in a cooler in the trunk of your car along with a few frozen ice packs.)

238. Shop in bulk. Even if you don't have enough space at home to store the items, you can still save time and money and split the order with a family member or friend.

12.

Cooking

239. Use your slow cooker. You may be surprised at the quality of the meals that can be made with a slow cooker. (Save even more time and purchase a slow cooker with a pull-out pot that goes directly on the stove, in the oven, and in the microwave.)

240. Love mangos? Don't waste another minute trying to cut around the odd-shaped pit; instead buy a mango splitter. Save time peeling a tomato by gently rubbing the back of a knife all over it before peeling. Peel garlic faster by placing the flat side of a knife on the clove of garlic and giving it a quick hit; the garlic will come right out of the peel. Picking up a few of these quick cooking tips from cooking shows, cooking websites, or cookbooks can save you time when cooking your favorite meals.

241. When hard-boiling eggs, put a drop or two of food coloring in the water; you can easily tell uncooked and hard-boiled eggs apart by noting whether or not their shells are tinted. No more wasting time trying to figure out which are still raw ones or spending time cleaning up a mess if you guess wrong.

242. Keep the tools you need for your most frequent tasks handy. Hang cooking utensils near the stove. Keep extra garbage bags near the garbage can. Move things to make it less time-consuming to reach for them.

243. Set up a containing station where you can quickly find the items you need for wrapping, storing, and containing food. Have plastic wrap, aluminum foil, baggies, and plastic containers on hand nearby.

244. Covering a pot of water will make it boil faster, and covering food as it cooks will make it cook faster. Slicing meat lengthwise (known as butterflying) speeds up cooking time as well.

245. Instead of buying take-out dinners on busy nights, try cooking a frozen dinner or a ready-made meal from the grocery store. Take-out is not always the timesaver it appears to be. If you spend twenty minutes driving to and from the restaurant and another ten minutes in line, you could have microwaved a frozen lasagna in that amount of time.

246. Don't fry your bacon—microwave it instead. Line a plate with paper towels; place your bacon on the towels and cover it with another layer of towels, then microwave. Cleanup is easy, and crisp bacon is guaranteed in less than half the time.

247. Use a microwave splatter guard over food when you are reheating it. The less splatter there is, the less time you have to spend cleaning. Also use a splatter guard when frying on the stove.

248. Consider lining your stove and oven floor with aluminum foil for quick cleanup in the event of spills and splatters. (Avoid laying the foil across the vents, as that would stop the heat from circulating properly.)

249. Mix pancake batter in your blender; then pour directly onto the griddle. You'll have smooth batter and less to clean up. (Clean the blender by putting dish soap and water in the blender and blending it. Rinse and you are done.)

250. Whenever you can, opt to use the toaster oven; food cooks faster and saves you time. (Not all food can be cooked in a toaster oven, so be sure to read the preparation guidelines.)

251. Use a portable timer; don't be a slave to the stove. Free yourself from the built-in oven timer by buying a small, battery-operated or dial oven timer. Take it with you out to the garden or to the home office so you don't have to stay in the kitchen while your food cooks.

252. Funnels can make jobs easier and save you time since there will be less spillage. You can use them to pour bulk items into smaller containers, such as filling saltshakers.

253. Use an egg separator or a small funnel to quickly separate an egg. The white will go through, while the yolk will stay behind.

254. Instead of icing cupcakes individually, place cupcakes in rows close to one another and then ice the entire top.

255. Save time frosting a cake by sprinkling it with a bag of chocolate or peanut butter chips while the cake is still warm. In just a few minutes, the chips will melt and be easy to spread. (You can add a few mini marshmallows to the chips as well to create swirled icing.)

256. Use just one measuring cup to measure more than one ingredient at a time. For example, if you need one half cup of sugar and one half cup of flour, use the one cup measure for both, filling it halfway with sugar and then topping it off with the flour. (This is especially helpful if you opt for microwave-safe measuring cups; that way you can melt butter directly in the cup and then add the rest of the ingredients for easy mixing.)

257. Make cleanup faster when cooking or baking by spraying the cooking surface with non-stick spray.

258. Make and freeze all the foods that store well, like pancakes, lasagna, browned ground beef, stews, chopped onions, and cooked rice, just to name a few. Sauces can be frozen in ice cube trays and then popped out to use as needed.

259. Precut the vegetables you'll need for the next day or so. Dice the onions, press the garlic, and chop the celery. (Most stay freshest wrapped in aluminum foil.)

260. Use a sharp knife; you will be able to cut things more quickly and more easily. Plus, you lessen your chances of injuring yourself; a dull knife is much more dangerous to work with.

261. Designate and label one pair of scissors as kitchen food scissors. Cutting scallions and herbs, opening packages, and so many other kitchen tasks are just easier with scissors.

262. Layer wax paper between meats, like pork chops and fish, *before* freezing them. That way you can take out only as much as you need to cook. (This works well if you shop in bulk and buy very large portions; you can easily separate these into family-sized servings.)

263. Clean as you go. Almost everything is easier to clean up before it dries. (It can be really helpful, especially when baking, to put a dishpan in the sink filled with hot water and dish soap to soak measuring spoons and mixer beaters.)

HAVE MORE TIME TODAY!

1. Make meal planning more manageable by starting out with just one week of your new meal plan and adding on.
2. Choose two items that you can get delivered and order them today.
3. Experiment to find one dish everyone likes that is prepared in the slow cooker, and make it at least once a month to free up one night of cooking.

TRY THIS:

Remove one cooking utensil from your drawer that you never use and give it away; the less you have to look through, the faster you can find what you need.

REPEAT AFTER ME:

"I'm okay with the fact that I choose not to serve a five-course meal every day. My realistic goal is to serve balanced meals throughout the week."

Part Five:

Getting It Done

Between running to the bank, shopping for pet food, returning library books, and stopping at three stores to find the gift you want to buy for the party this weekend, it's no wonder you don't have any time left. And that doesn't even cover things that come up last minute. So are you just going to resign yourself to the fact that this is how it's always been and assume this is the way it will always be? Or are you ready to take back your time and reclaim your weekends?

13.

Errands

264. Create a leaving station nearest to the door that you use most often. This station is where you will store the items you need for the week; for example, bills to be mailed, library books to return, and coupons for the stores you will stop into. Other items include your cell phone and charger and your keys. A leaving station can be one shelf of an armoire or bookcase in your entryway, or even a bench or basket.

265. Another item to store at your leaving station is an in/out tote bag. This tote bag is different than your briefcase, purse, or diaper bag. This tote bag is used only on the days when you have errands to run. Toss everything you need inside, and be on your way.

266. To avoid rewriting your information over and over on forms, carry return address labels with you, and whenever you are asked to provide your name and address, just stick one on the paper.

267. Group your errands together. If you are not in a rush to get to a particular store, wait a few days until you have to go to some other store nearby.

268. When you have a list of a few errands to run, try not to leave your least favorite stop until the end. You will be tempted to skip the stop and leave it for another day. But if you start with the least pleasant, leaving a fun stop until the end, then you will be much more likely to do everything. Plus, if you factor in a little extra time to enjoy your favorite stop, then running that errand is more like a reward for a job well-done. For example, if you have to pick up a book as a gift and you like to browse in bookstores, then leave enough time to look around while you're there.

269. Consider something new. The fact that you have always shopped at a particular store doesn't mean you must *keep* shopping there. Consider whether there might be a more convenient store with longer hours or more parking. If so, it might make sense to switch. (Of course, you will have to try the store out to be sure they carry what you need. It is not a time-saver if you can buy most of your items there but still need to make an additional stop to get one last item from another store.)

270. Don't stray from your usual stores for larger shopping trips or specialty items, since you will not know the layout of the new store or even if that store carries the items you want to buy. If the store does not have your brand or exactly what you want, you will end up wasting more time.

271. Save time searching for your car in the parking lot by always parking in the same row of the parking lot at the stores you frequent. Instituting that simple habit will save you lots of time.

272. When you park in a large lot, like at a stadium, jot down the row and aisle you are in. Place the note in your wallet so you can find the note and easily locate your car. Or if you prefer, add "car" to your cell phone address book, and then whenever you need to, plug in the aisle number or letter.

273. When plotting out your errands, start with the one farthest from your home and then work back towards your house. (The exception is if you are buying something like frozen food in summer that will not last in the car as you make your other stops.)

274. Instead of spending time and money stopping for a drink or a snack while out running errands, take a small, insulated lunch bag with you, filled with a snack and a drink.

275. Stop wasting time standing in line at the post office to buy stamps. Instead, order them online and have them delivered through www.usps.com or buy them at the grocery store checkout or ATM machine. (If you ship a lot of packages from your home, you can even print the postage out at your computer after weighing the package and then call for a pick up.)

14.
Appointments

276. Always bring something to work on when you go to an appointment. That way if there is a delay and you are left waiting, you can use the time wisely. Bring something to read, thank-you notes to write, knitting, photos and a photo album to slide them into; the list is endless. (To make them easier to transport, put all the items in a single tote bag and carry the tote bag with you on the days when you might have a little time to "waste.")

277. When making an appointment, ask for the very first appointment of the day. This means less time waiting since schedules get more behind as the day goes by.

278. You can also ask for the first appointment right after the lunch break. Most places stop for lunch, which allows them to catch up, so the first appointment after lunch usually starts on time.

279. Ask if you can make an appointment outside regular hours. You might be surprised to find out your hairdresser has no problem giving you an appointment at seven in the morning, which would allow you to get your hair cut before having to commute to work. You won't know if you don't ask.

280. Be sure to call ahead and confirm that the appointment is still on as scheduled. (Save even more time by putting the phone number right next to the appointment on your calendar.)

281. Call right before you leave to confirm they are running on time. For example, if it takes you fifteen minutes to get to your physician's office, call right before you are ready to walk out the door to ask if they are ready for you. If not, you can spend a few more minutes at home, rather than wasting time sitting in a waiting room.

282. Save time looking for the address. Know where you are going before you set out. Get clear directions with landmarks and a picture of the place; also ask for a landmark that will tell you if you went too far.

15.

Shopping

283. Pick brands before you go shopping. You can waste a lot of time standing in the toothpaste or tissue aisle trying to make a decision.

284. Do your research before you go out to make a big purchase. You will save lots of time if you already know the questions to ask and the options available.

285. Decide what you want before you go to buy an outfit. Look online or cut out a picture from a magazine or catalog so you know what you are looking for.

286. Call ahead to ask if the store has what you are looking for. If they do, ask if they can put it behind the register for you. (It is important to ask the employee for his or her name; they will be more likely to actually check the shelf to be sure they have the item in stock and then you will know who to ask for if the item is not behind the register.)

287. Instead of wasting time walking around the store looking for the item, take a moment to ask an employee where it is located in the store.

288. Save time looking for the coupons, gift cards, or credit slips for a particular store. Use a pocket-size accordion folder and write on the tabs the names of the stores (or store sections like clothes, food, toys) you frequent most; then store coupons, gift cards, or credit slips in the appropriate pocket. If your purse is too small to carry the file with you, store it in the glove box or console of your car. (This is also helpful if you return items frequently and need to keep the receipts handy.)

289. Instead of shopping in person for a gift for someone, shop online or by catalog and have the item shipped directly to the giftee. In many cases, companies will gift wrap the item and enclose a note.

290. Hire a baby-sitter to watch your children while you shop. If you already have a sitter scheduled to come, spend a few extra minutes running errands before you return home. If a baby-sitter is out of your budget, consider bartering with a friend or neighbor; you'll run a few errands for him or her while you are out and he or she will watch the children.

291. Keep a few generic last-minute gifts on hand to use in a pinch. Art sets for children, candle sets for hostesses, and a receiving blanket for a newborn all work well. Of course, don't choose items that have an expiration date like many gift cards and food items. (This idea will only work if you remember you have the gifts, so designate one shelf, basket, or drawer for them and replenish it as often as necessary.)

292. Shopping online or by catalog can save you time, but only if the store is reputable and the item is one you don't need to see in person. If the item never arrives or if you need to mail it back, it is not a time savings at all. Items like shoes can be difficult to judge without trying them on; for clothing, you won't necessarily know the quality of the item or you might not like the feel of the fabric. On the other hand, paper towels, stationery, and pet food are easy items to purchase without having to see them in person. (Once you have had success with a particular retailer, remember that store and the brand you like. Knowing that makes shopping in the future less time-consuming.)

293. When shopping online, save time searching for passwords and login information by keeping a list under the computer's keyboard. Try choosing a single password that will fit most requirements. For example, many passwords now require six to ten characters with a minimum of two numbers. Choose a password that fits that criteria and use it for most login needs, and you can abbreviate it for any login that requires a shorter password. Having one password that is not easy for others to guess makes life a lot easier and saves you lots of time.

294. Think auto delivery. Whenever you can, put items you consistently use on automatic delivery. By scheduling automatic delivery of things like pet food, bottled water, paper towels, and printer paper, you can save time buying the items and carting them home. You also avoid the risk of running out.

295. As soon as you get home, take your purchases out of the bags and put them away. This prevents you from spending time looking around for things you just bought that are concealed in a mountain of plastic bags.

296. Whenever you need to shop to replace an odd item, take the old one with you—it makes shopping a lot easier. You can ask for assistance, and instead of trying to describe it, the person helping you will be able to see it. (If you are sending someone shopping in your place, it can help to send the old box or packaging from the item with him or her as the example of what to buy. There are so many options, even for something as simple as tissues; it is much easier to match the package than it is to spend time reading the fine print.)

HAVE MORE TIME TODAY!

1. Group your errands together instead of running out multiple times for one or two things.
2. Always confirm appointments, and take something to do with you in case you have spare time.
3. Before you shop, call ahead to the store and ask if they have the item in stock.

TRY THIS:

Create a leaving station this week.

REPEAT AFTER ME:

"I take my purchases out of the bag as soon as I come in the door."

Part Six:

Speed Cleaning

Raise your hand if you like to clean. Anyone? While it is true that sometimes cleaning can be a cathartic thing to do, most of the time we do not look forward to it. Even if you do like to clean, you can pick up a few quick tricks that will make the process go a little faster so you have more time for other things you enjoy.

16.

Zone Clean

297. Stop wearing shoes in the house. Eighty-seven percent of the dirt that comes into your home is tracked in on the bottom of your shoes; by taking your shoes off at the door, you greatly reduce your cleaning regimen.

298. Store cleaning supplies in the rooms where you use them. That may mean having duplicates in the house, but it saves time. Instead of running from room to room to gather up the supplies, you can have them on hand where you need them.

299. Multitasking cleaners save time, since you won't have to cart around lots of products or open and close lots of containers.

300. Whenever possible, pretreat the area. Allow the product to work while you attend to something else. (Set a timer to remind yourself to come back and finish the job. If you wait too long, the cleaner dries and it takes twice as long to clean.)

301. Use the right tool for the job. For example, an old toothbrush can help you to clean behind the faucet so you won't have to waste time trying to shove a rag into such a tight spot. (Putting socks over your hands and using them for polishing and dusting is a great trick.)

302. Go for the good stuff. Paper products and cleaning solutions are not the place to skimp. To save time, money, and the environment, try creating homemade solutions from ingredients you probably already have around your home, such as white vinegar, baking soda, and lemon juice. (Recipes for mixing up your own household cleaners can be found in the resource section of this book or on www.jamienovak.com.)

303. Keep it simple! It can be tempting to try the newest cleaning gadget. Some are worth the time and effort, but more often than not, the items don't work as well as advertised, or an item may take so much time to learn how to use or to clean that you are better off just doing the job without it. Sometimes baking soda and water work better than anything else.

304. Carry the tools of the trade with you; sticking everything in a small bucket with a handle or a plastic caddy works well. (Sometimes it can even be a timesaver to wear an apron with pockets so you can have the items you need within arms' reach.)

305. Worrying about getting your hands dirty makes cleaning tasks take much longer, so wear gloves. You'll do a more thorough job and won't have to do it again as soon.

306. Break up cleaning into small tasks; for example, instead of cleaning the entire refrigerator top to bottom, clean a single shelf at a time. You don't have to wait until you have big blocks of time to clean; you can integrate cleaning into your daily life.

307. Speed-cleaning is much easier when you have less to clean around. Avoid large collections of knickknacks and try to keep countertops as clear as possible; canister sets, toasters, and piles of mail interfere with a speedy touch-up.

308. When you do need to leave items out, try putting them on trays, so you can lift a single tray to clean instead of having to pick up each item individually.

309. Try to avoid purchasing special care items such as sterling silver that will need polishing or knives that cannot be put in the dishwasher.

310. If it is within your budget, opt for the heavy-duty spring and fall house-cleaning to be done by a professional cleaning company. They have the tools and supplies to do the job, and they are usually better at it. (Remember: You don't need to have them come in and do the entire house; if you prefer to delegate just the washing of the windows and the cleaning of the vents, they can do just that.)

IT WORKED FOR HER

"One thing I learned from my mother was to use plastic shopping bags to line small trash cans. I even put several in [the trash can], one on top of the other, so when one is full I don't have to replace it. I just lift it out and another one is underneath."

Sandra B.

311. Make the task of cleaning as fun as possible. Try turning on music or deciding to read the next chapter in the book you've been wanting to get to *after* you finish your task for the day.

312. If you are trying to locate a dropped item like an earring or simply trying not to vacuum up small items, fasten nylon over the vacuum nozzle.

313. If it's not dirty, then don't clean it. This one may seem obvious. But you'd be surprised how much time you may be wasting cleaning and re-cleaning before it is really necessary.

314. Stop over cleaning; once the area is clean leave it alone. Spending 20 percent more effort to perfect it is not necessary.

315. More is not always better; only use the amount of cleaning solution you need. Using too much means wasting time cleaning the cleaning solution!

316. When you are vacuuming, instead of rolling over that stubborn piece of lint that refuses to be sucked, just bend down and pick it up!

317. When refilling one container, take an extra moment and fill them all. For example, when refilling the liquid soap dispenser at one sink, go to the others and top them off as well since you already have the supplies out.

318. If you notice something running low, replace the item before it runs out, since it usually takes longer to replace the item in a rush when you need it. For example, when you notice the toilet paper roll is running low, replace it with a new one and leave the replaced roll on top to be used up first.

319. To quickly clean stuck-on food from the inside of the microwave, boil a cup of water in the microwave. The steam will help loosen dried-on gunk, making it easy to wipe away. You can even add a bit of lemon juice for a fresh scent.

320. Make cleaning as enjoyable as possible. Hide spare change around for children to find while they clean.

321. When filling the dishwasher, put in the dishes in a way that it takes less time to match them up and put them away once they are clean. (Doing this with spoons is the one exception, since they can nest together and won't come out as clean.)

322. Once you clean the windows in your house, spray car-windshield rain-repellent on the outside of them to keep the dirt off and streaks from appearing.

17.
Simple Kitchen Cleanup

323. Use your dishwasher for more than just dishes. Clean shower caddies, pet dishes, soap holders, and so much more. If the item is small, contain it in a net bag so it does not fall into the motor. Use the air-dry option for rubber and plastic items.

324. Wipe up spills in the refrigerator as soon as they happen, and while you are at it, take an extra moment and run the cleaning cloth over another shelf or along the outside handle. It is faster to do it when you have the supplies already out, and there will be less to do later.

325. Line the shelves and the drawers of the refrigerator; it is quicker to pull up the lining than it is to remove the entire shelf to clean it.

326. Put plates under potentially messy items, like defrosting meat, to avoid spills and drips. The less mess there is, the less time you'll have to spend cleaning up.

327. Contain marinades and condiments in a shallow caddy; that way if something spills, the mess will be contained to the caddy. You'll also save time looking for the items in the refrigerator.

328. Toss out or recycle the extra disposable take-out containers, drinking mugs, and condiment packages you've collected. The less you have to sort through to find the ones you actually use, the more time you save.

329. As you cook, rinse dirty utensils, pots, and pans, then put them in the dishwasher. That way, when you sit down to eat you can enjoy the meal instead of staring at dirty pots and pans; plus, if the dishwasher is full, it can run as you eat, so the dishes from the meal have a place to go when you are finished eating.

330. When you're ready to run the dishwasher but it is only half full, add burner covers, a spoon rest, or small shelves from the refrigerator so those can get cleaned as well.

331. Whenever you can, opt to purchase items that are dishwasher safe; this will save you lots of time you would otherwise spend cleaning items by hand.

332. Bendable cutting boards can save you time when prepping meals. Instead of chopping vegetables and then having to spend time moving the food from one place to another, you can mold the cutting board into a U-shape and slide the food right where you want it.

333. Enlist help. Make it a household rule that you and others will clean spills as soon as they happen and that dirty dishes will be put directly into the dishwasher. You can also delegate some of the time-consuming chores, like emptying the recycling and taking out the garbage.

18.

Cleaning
Made Easy

334. Store a floor duster with disposable cloths in a closet near the bathroom. It will be easy to grab the duster and go over the floor during the week.

335. If you use disposable makeup cloths to wash your face; rinse and reuse them to quick-clean the sink and counter or spot clean the floor.

336. After your family members finish brushing their teeth or shaving, use a dry terrycloth hand towel on the mirror and bathroom faucets to wipe away spots of lather so they won't build up.

337. Before getting out of the shower, run a squeegee down the shower tiles and door. Although this may seem to cost you more time, in the long run you will spend less time cleaning.

338. After you flush the toilet, sprinkle 1/4 cup of baking soda into the wet bowl. Take your shower, and then give the bowl a single scrub. Flush to rinse.

IT WORKED FOR HER

"I use Woolite on a wet cloth to clean soap scum, mineral deposits, etc., off the bathroom porcelain and chrome. No need to scrub! Yeah! For stubborn mineral deposits on the faucets, I leave the wet Woolite cloth or sponge on the stain and come back later. I also discovered that the sink I soaked my delicates in was always sparkling. Unconventional, sure, but it works!"

Dorothy Bellow, S. Plainfield, NJ

339. Keep your large vacuum on the main level of the home or the level with the most rooms where you use it. Then store a stick-vac on the other levels of your home. This means you can avoid lugging the large vacuum up and down stairs for spills or spruce-ups in between deep cleanings.

340. Be diligent about weeding magazines and catalogs. Make it a weekly routine to sort through the basket of magazines and catalogs. Recycle the duplicate catalogs, and toss magazines (read or unread) after three months. It takes longer to sort though larger stacks, so be sure to tackle the pile weekly. The fewer catalogs and magazines you have coming into your home, the less time it will take to deal with them; end your subscriptions to the ones that you don't read. If you don't want to waste the remainder of the subscription, you can call the office and request a change of address to have it sent to a local hospital, nursing home, day care, salon, library, physician's office, friend, neighbor, or relative; the options are endless.

341. Toss the junk mail *daily*. The longer you let it pile up, the longer it will take to sort through it. Make it a habit to bring the mail in when you have time to sort it; then take a moment and toss the junk mail immediately.

IT WORKED FOR HER

"Keep a wastebasket by the front door for all the junk mail. Get rid of it fast!"

Lisette G.

342. If you prefer to shred the mail that contains sensitive information, keep the shredder plugged in at a handy location and shred the mail immediately. Avoid making a "to be shred" pile. Just shred right then or rip and toss. (If you have a backlog of shredding to get caught up on, you can save time by delegating the task to a family member or even the baby-sitter once the children have gone to bed. You can even hire the sitter for a one-time shredding project. You can also place the items to be shredded into a bag and then cover it with an unpleasant substance, such as a splash of bleach.)

343. Before you go to bed, do a quick pick-up of the living room. Collect the remote controls and place them in a basket or a single drawer. Straighten the magazine/newspaper basket, fold throw blankets, put throw pillows back on the couch, and put away DVDs and CDs. It takes a lot less time to do a speedy job daily rather than spend hours at the end of the week.

344. You don't have to waste lots of time searching for the music CD you want to play. But you also don't have to spend hours alphabetizing your music collection either. Instead, group your CDs by category and contain each group in its own bin or shelf. (Most tissue box covers turned upside down fit CDs perfectly; measure first to be sure, but this can be a decorative way to store and display your CDs.)

345. Before you walk out of your bedroom in the morning, grab any stray items from your dresser top and nightstand that do not belong there—glasses of water, receipts, and other items that will pile up and require extra time later to clean.

346. When you take off your clothing, hang it up right away or put it directly in the dirty hamper; the floor or the arm of a chair are not options. (Designate one area of your closet for the items that have been worn but do not yet need to be laundered. You may get more than one wear out of your jeans—just put them away in between.)

347. Put stuff in the right place the first time. When you take off your jewelry, put it in its box right away. There is no sense putting it down, then having to move it a few times before you finally put it away. If it is not put away, you'll have to spend time hunting for it the next time you need it.

348. To save steps when making beds, store extra sets of sheets between the mattress and the box spring. Or if you prefer, place them on a shelf in your closet; if you are short on space in the closet, opt for an ottoman or trunk at the foot of your bed with a lift up top and storage inside.

349. Hang a paper-towel holder on the inside of the bathroom cabinet door so you can grab a towel to spot clean.

350. A pumice stone will take unsightly stains off the toilet bowl without scratching the porcelain. (I suggest that you test it in an unseen area first, but to date no bowl I know of has been scratched!)

NINETEEN HOUSEHOLD TASKS YOU CAN DO IN FIVE MINUTES OR LESS

351. Wipe handprints from the fridge.

352. Toss outdated food.

353. Wipe off sticky shelves.

354. Line the fruit and vegetable drawer with paper towels.

355. Tuck marinades and other sticky jars into foil-lined muffin cups.

356. Change the bed linens.

357. Fold a few clothes.

358. Mend one thing.

359. Swish toilet bowl.

360. Spray tiles to pretreat.

361. Empty the garbage.

362. Take out the recycling.

363. Toss wrinkled clothes into the dryer, and then hang them to avoid ironing.

364. Take one appliance that you don't use off the counter to save time cleaning around it.

365. Unload the dishwasher and put glasses and plates in the nearest cabinet.

366. Conduct a five-minute pick-up every night with entire family.

367. Spray the oven to pretreat.

368. Dust an area of a room.

369. Shred a pile of junk mail.

HAVE MORE TIME TODAY!

1. Store the cleaning supplies where you use them.
2. Clear the kitchen countertops of unnecessary items to make cleaning easier.
3. Designate one place for the remote controls to be stored.

TRY THIS:

Make a cleaning caddy today and find a place to store it.

REPEAT AFTER ME:

"I always improve a room as I go."

Part Seven:

A Parent's Life

Do you ever just want the world to stop so you can catch up? You are not alone! Remember that doing everything yourself is actually selfish. At some point, other family members will need to know how to do what you do, and by not showing them, you are putting them at a disadvantage. Ask for help when you need it—this is not a sign of weakness. And take the time to show others how things are done; this is very important. Showing children how to manage their time now means years from now they will not be reading this book or attending one of my workshops.

19.
Children

370. Take time to show your children how to create schedules and teach them other time-management strategies. Work with them to create their own schedules and allow them to carry out that schedule on their own; children learn by doing. This means that you will be able to delegate more and more to them, and years from now, your child will not have to borrow this book, since they will already know how to stay on top of things.

371. Use a calendar to write in due dates, like library book return dates and school project and book report due dates; then break it up and show the children how to do a little at a time. This helps them to learn how to plan—an incredibly valuable life skill!

372. Stop running around the house looking for the library books and movies you need to return. Designate one basket or shelf where you will store the borrowed items.

373. Let each child be a special helper of the day. Take your monthly calendar and write the initial of one child per day, rotating each day. Then every day you will know which child to call on to help out. This will eventually save you lots of time since each child will become equally skilled in all the tasks. (Even if the way they do the task is not up to your standards, allow them to help anyway.)

374. Storing your children's artwork in unused pizza boxes is a way to clearly store each child's art separately, so you don't have to spend time sifting through bags of it.

375. By scanning the calendar of events for the month, you will become better able to plan for special events. For example, purchasing a gift in advance of an upcoming birthday party or washing the school logo T-shirt to wear on school spirit day.

376. Scanning the calendar at the start of each week helps you prepare for any special events that week in advance.

377. Keep as many art project pieces on hand as possible—empty shoe boxes, poster board, small plastic figurines for 3D projects, etc. With these items on hand, you will not have to spend time running to the store.

378. Having a single location for all incoming school papers is a great way to keep them organized so you can find them when you need them.

379. For the papers that need to be retuned to school the next day, like a signed report card or permission slip, take a single magnetic clip and call it the "today clip." Place it on the front of the refrigerator for those papers; teach each child to check the today clip when packing his or her backpack.

380. Stop wasting time running around looking for glue sticks and other supplies your children need to complete their homework. Instead, give each child a small basket filled with one of each type of homework supply he or she needs. Label the homework bins and place extra supplies out of reach. You can then shop at home to refill the bins as needed.

381. Use a timer to keep on track. Set it to buzz as a reminder for the children that it is time to clean up and get ready to leave, or as a gentle reminder for other things throughout the day.

382. Write your hospital and pediatrician's number on a piece of paper, along with other emergency contact numbers. Hang the paper near the phone so it is handy should you ever need to use it. Also, take a moment to add the numbers to your cell phone address book since you never know where you might be when you need them—not only in the event of an emergency, but also to call to confirm an appointment, say you are running late, or ask if the paperwork you need is ready to be picked up.

383. One way to stop wasting time cleaning up after your children is to designate a box as "clutter jail." Give the children a reminder that they have five minutes to clean up; you can even set a timer. Once the buzzer rings, place anything that is left out in clutter jail. To retrieve an item from clutter jail, your child can help out with another chore or task—a fair trade of time since it took your time to collect the left out item(s). Usually it just takes one episode during which something they care about is locked up in clutter jail for children to follow the cleanup rule. (When the jail starts to get too crowded, you can select unclaimed items to toss and/or have an amnesty day on which items can be sprung without penalty.)

384. Try a new family rule of only allowing two extracurricular activities per season. This not only saves you time and money, but helps your children learn to make choices while getting good at one or two things, rather than spreading themselves too thin and being just average at lots of stuff.

385. Set up a carpool. It may take a little time to coordinate an initial schedule, but once it is done, it is a daily timesaver! Use the carpools for more than just rides to and from school; also use them for birthday parties, playdates, and extracurricular activities. (Be sure to save all the carpool parents' names and numbers in your cell phone in case you are out and need to get in touch with one of them.)

386. Print "mom" business cards with all your important information on them. You can list your contact information, the children's pediatrician, any allergies or special instructions regarding your children, and anything else you need other parents to have when they are caring for your kids. This keeps you from having to write it out each time. (Visit www.jamienovak.com for more information on these cards.)

387. If you find your child complains about his or her chore so much that you think it would be easier to just do it yourself, then try rotating the chores so they don't become bored with the routine.

388. Stop wasting time and money buying duplicates of items that you already own for one child and that are suitable to save as hand-me-downs for the next child. The key is to store them in clearly labeled containers so you can find them when you need them.

389. Tuck away toys your children have not used in a few weeks or longer. If you throw them out or give them away, they might be missed. Instead, place them in a box, clearly label the box, and tuck them away for another month or two. If they are missed, you can bring them out of storage, and if they are not missed, you can part with them.

390. Save time repeating yourself by making sure you have your child's full attention before giving instructions. Make eye contact, be precise, and ask the child to repeat back what you said to clear up any miscommunications immediately.

391. Keep a clipboard in the car with a pen attached to it. Clip on a list of the phone numbers for your children's classmates, coaches, pediatricians, along with other commonly referenced phone numbers. (Use a highlighter to highlight commonly dialed numbers, like those of your child's favorite friends on the class list. The clipboard in the car can double as a writing surface to fill out thank-you cards, write out bills, or fill out forms in the car while waiting for your children.)

392. Since most forms require you to fill in similar information such as Social Security numbers, driver's license numbers, and insurance ID numbers, keep a copy of a recently filled-out form handy. Then the next time you need to fill out a form, you can copy from the master instead of looking up the information all over again. (A great place to keep this master form is in a sheet protector glued to the back of the clipboard so you won't waste time looking for it the next time you need it.)

393. Consolidate appointments. For example, make two simultaneous haircut appointments with two beauticians so both children can have their hair cut at the same time. If simultaneous appointments won't work, try for at least back-to-back, so you can go half as often.

394. Allow distractions while remaining focused. It is unrealistic to think you can have uninterrupted blocks of time when the children are home. So learn to stop, remember where you left off, do something else, and get right back to what you were doing. For example, stop paying bills, grab a snack for your child, and then go right back to paying bills as if the interruption never happened. (It can be helpful to leave yourself a little note as a reminder of where you left off so you can get right back into it without wasting time reviewing what you've already done.)

395. Limit your child's social engagements. Accepting all the invitations your child receives to attend birthday parties and playdates, coupled with all the extracurricular activities he or she wants to participate in, such as scouting, sports, and dance, can make everyone feel overwhelmed. Limiting the number of social engagements and extracurricular activities you will accept saves time and also allows your child to experience one or two things fully instead of being shuttled between five or six activities that he or she doesn't get a lot out of.

396. Have your child record the notes from school on a tape recorder that he or she can listen to while showering, playing games, or doing other tasks. Recording them helps your child retain the information at a much higher rate, which means less time spent quizzing your child or reviewing homework.

397. If your children are like most, they have different routines for being picked up from school or day care different days of the week. To minimize confusion and to avoid mistakes and lost time, create clips that display a different picture of the options your child has; for example, a bus, a car, and one of your neighbors or carpool members. Then, each night as you prepare for the next day, clip the correct clip to your children's backpacks. That way they will always know where to go and who is going to pick them up.

398. Do you ever wish there could be a clone of you? It is not uncommon to be needed in two or even three places at one time. Considering the number of demands on your time, it's bound to happen. The single best way to avoid double-booking your calendar is to write everything down and to check it often. When it does happen, whether due to double-booking or the necessities of your schedule, attempt to resolve it the best you can by compromising. For example, you might be able to skip Back-to-School Night by making a lunchtime appointment to meet your child's teacher, or you might be able to have someone videotape an event (like a soccer game) for you to watch later. But don't over-compromise; you may be tempted to try to squeeze two events in by leaving one early and arriving late to the other, but that will not serve anyone's best interest.

20.

Special Needs Children

399. To help your child remember the routines, make charts using pictures of your child doing the tasks, like brushing teeth or putting on shoes. Use a few pictures in a row to make a visual picture of the routine.

400. Use a timer to help you and your child stay focused on the one task you are working on for a specific block of time. Using a timer helps to eliminate distractions and allows you both to focus on the task at hand.

401. To save you time in the long run, take a little time to label things around the house with signs. You can use words and pictures depending on which your child will be better able to understand. Labeling sock drawers, the cabinet the dinner plates are kept in, and the basket that holds his or her favorite movies will save your child lots of time hunting for them. Even labeling shoes with "R" and "L" for right and left can be a huge timesaver.

402. Avoid wasting time looking for test results and progress reports. Keep them in a central location so you can access them quickly. If you need to carry the reports with you to and from appointments, then an accordion folder or traveling file box with a hanging folder might be the answer. However, if you mostly just need to keep them in the house, then a single file drawer might work well.

403. Keeping a single three-ring binder filled with sheet protectors will make it easy to tuck away contact lists for the physicians, therapists, and counselors, along with directions to the offices and any brochures, business cards, and other necessary information. Note: Putting a three-ring pencil pouch in the front will give you a perfect place to store a pen and other miscellaneous items.

404. Another three-ring binder prefilled with clear plastic sheet protectors is a great place to store suggested activities and exercises given to you to do with your child in between appointments.

405. Insurance claim forms can take a long time to fill out. So if you need to submit your own claim forms to the insurance companies, take one and fill it in with all the generic information like name, address, and primary physician. Then make photocopies of the form and keep them handy. Next time you need one, most of the work will already be done. And to help you keep track of payments due to you, keep a running list and mark them off as they arrive.

21.
New Baby

406. Bath time can take twice as long when you have to spend time running around looking for the supplies and toys. Try keeping a basket in the bathroom filled with bath supplies like: towels, washcloths, shampoo, soap, lotions, diapers, wipes, toys, and a book to read. Note: Short on space to store a basket? Go with an over-the-door clear plastic shoe holder and use the clear pockets to store the supplies so they are on hand at bath time.

407. Keep a filled diaper bag in the car so you have what you need on hand and won't have to make a trip to the store in emergencies. Some items to consider stashing inside include: diapers, wipes, a supply of rash creams, sunscreen and insect repellent, fever reducer/pain reliever, antiseptic spray and antibiotic ointment, Band-Aids, spare outfits in a variety of weights for unexpected temperature changes, bottled water, formula if you use it, snacks that don't spoil and juice boxes, tweezers for splinters, a paint brush for wiping away sand, extra toys, and a pacifier (if your child uses one). Having this supply on hand prepares you for just about anything. (This emergency bag can easily be created using almost-empty tubes of ointments and bottles of things. When the tube of antibiotic ointment is almost used up, pop it in a ziplock bag and store it in the emergency bag.)

408. In addition to a changing station in your child's nursery, create mini-stations throughout your home. A decorative basket containing diapers, a toy, wipes, and a changing pad can save you time all day long.

409. Keep two or three duplicate diaper bags ready to go. If each one contains identical items, then whichever one you grab will have what you need. Be sure to refill when you get back home, and you'll always be prepared so you can get out the door faster.

HAVE MORE TIME TODAY!

1. Realize that your child(ren) are learning how to balance their time by duplicating what they see you do.
2. Create a binder to house all the paperwork you need to take with you on appointments.
3. Set up mini changing stations on each level of your home.

TRY THIS:

Teach your child one new skill this week by doing it together until he or she can do it independently.

REPEAT AFTER ME:

"I am a great parent."

Part Eight:

When It's Out of Your Control

Sometimes the ability to manage time is simply not in your control. But that does not mean that you just have to give up all together. Whether it is a friend, a family member, or a boss who put the crunch on your time, there are a number of tricks you can have up your sleeve to deal with the unexpected demands. And while there will be occasions when you'll simply have to buckle down and get through the busy time, you can handle it with grace and lay the groundwork to lessen the chances of it happening again.

22.

Spouse, Family, and Friends

410. The very first thing you need to do is grab the calendar and block out time that you and your spouse can use to go on dates. Without the time set aside to do fun things together, you can quickly lose that strong connection. Additionally, the time off enjoying life together will be important to help get you through the not-so-fun parts of the week, like getting through those long to-do lists and staying organized.

411. Teaming up with your spouse is the single best way to take back control of your time. If you have differences of opinion, you might find yourself working against each other. For example, if you want a free weekend a month and your spouse doesn't, then he or she might schedule couple or family events every weekend instead of leaving a weekend free. The key to success will be teaming up. There will have to be compromises made, but it will definitely be worth it in the end.

412. Place a single, ongoing master list on a computer spreadsheet or a whiteboard to avoid rewriting. If you both find it easier to work on the computer, then a shared real-time file might be the way to go. (Check out www.whiteboard.com for a free, password protected, online whiteboard.) You can both post comments for one another and update the file as well.

413. Setting deadlines that both you and your spouse agree on is a sure way to make things happen. Not only will you need a due date or deadline by which to complete the project, but you will also need interim deadlines to keep you on track. So if you want the garage cleared out by October, a yard sale in early September and buying shelving in mid-September would all be smaller goals that will help keep you on track for the October deadline. (Next to each task relating to the goal, it can be helpful to write the name of the person who is responsible for it, so you don't end up both working on the same task or letting something fall through the cracks.)

414. Miscommunication can account for a tremendous amount of wasted time. When someone does not clearly understand the instructions, the task may need to be redone. Communicate clearly; even go so far as to ask people to repeat back what they plan to do. That gives you a chance to catch anything that might need to be cleared up. Something as simple as sending your spouse to the store to pick up a book you want can turn into a time-wasting situation if he or she comes home with the wrong version of the book that you then need to go exchange.

415. Be precise. This falls under the "communicate clearly" heading. Asking your spouse to load your car with the bags to drop off for charity, and asking your spouse to put the three black bags for charity in the trunk of your car are two completely different statements. The first one is vague, and you might only find two of the three bags shoved into the front seat of your car. The second phrasing is precise enough to leave little room for error.

416. Figure out who is in charge of what. You may choose to be in charge of packing the lunches, and your spouse may be in charge of anything with batteries or light bulbs. So if your child comes to you with a toy that needs a battery replaced, that can automatically be delegated to your spouse. This saves time since each person can become skilled in specific areas, learn the short cuts, and know where the supplies for the projects are kept.

417. Stop redoing someone else's work. Unless there is a specific reason for why it has to be done a very particular way, leave it alone. Whether towels are rolled or folded is not a life-or-death decision. So, if someone else pitches in on a task and doesn't do it your way, try your best to leave it alone, remembering that your ultimate goal is not "perfectly" folded towels, it is more control over your time. Refolding towels is *not* the best use of your time.

418. Set up a lost-and-found bin, basket, or container. A single place where everyone in the house can toss something that they feel must be important but looks lost or out of place. Something that resembles the cover to a remote might be important, but at the moment that it is found, it may not be clear what it is or whom it might belong to. Instead of wasting time running around trying to figure out what it is or just tossing it in the garbage and then having to spend time and money to replace it, tuck it in the lost-and-found; then, when someone is looking for a plastic cover, they'll know where to look first.

419. Designate a drop zone for your spouse to use on his or her way in the door. A single place for keys, wallet or purse, loose change, and other papers like business cards and receipts. A drawer in an entryway table, a single shelf in the kitchen cabinet, or some other convenient location. Note: If the drop zone is not located right at the entrance of the home, there is less likelihood that it will be used.

23.

When You Have to Say Yes

420. Accept the job, but explain that it is putting you in a bad spot. Let whoever is asking know that you will need more notice the next time so you can come up with a suitable plan.

421. Agree to do it, but gently remind the asker that now he or she owes you one. Be sure to take them up on that favor in the near future. Often we feel too bad to collect from those that owe us favors, but doing so can really save you time when you are in a bind.

422. Offer a timetable when you accept the task. Having a clear deadline early on will help you to avoid last-minute pushes to complete the job.

423. Don't be afraid to ask for an extension. If you took the project on because no one else could or would, then it is possible you'll need more time to complete it. Don't be afraid to go back and say that you need more time. Just be fair and give them ample notice in case they have an absolute deadline and choose to do it themselves.

424. Take on the project, but request assistance. Simply explain that you can do X and Y but you'll have to turn it back over to them for Z.

425. Say yes, but offer a condition such as, "I can do this, but I can only give you three hours a week." Setting that limit in advance can be very helpful once you get into the project and have to remind the person that you only have limited amounts of time to devote to the job.

426. Accept the job, but remind the person that the completed job may not be up to your usual high standards since you are working under pressure. That way you will not feel compelled to spend endless hours making it perfect, and you can feel good about turning in work that is good but not great.

427. To help minimize the opportunity to have your time volunteered for you, choose your activities early before there is a last-minute call for help so you already have a committed position of your choosing that may take less time and be more fun for you. Let's say you belong to an organization in which everyone is required to play a role in the holiday party. Volunteering to send out the reminder emails might be a good choice since you can do it from home on your own time, and it is not that labor intensive. But if you wait until the party-planning meeting to volunteer, you might feel obligated to say yes when asked to take over the co-chairing duties that no one else would accept.

24.

Chronic Lateness and Adult AD/HD

428. Chronic lateness can be the result of the most well-intentioned thought: "I don't want to waste a single minute." You'll do projects and tasks right up until the last minute, sometimes overshooting your goal and then running super-late because you've lost track of time. Wanting to use every minute is a great goal, but how about deciding to leave the house early enough to arrive on time and taking something with you to work on in case you arrive early? That way you are using your minutes wisely, and you will also be where you need to be on time.

429. Not-so-hot planning can be the cause of some chronic lateness. You may recall with fondness that day the stars aligned and you made it to work in record time, no red lights, no bad weather, and only open road in front of you, but that cannot be your gauge. It's faulty. Instead, assume things will go wrong like construction, bad weather, or getting lost; then when it is a smooth ride, you'll be early; if not, you'll still be on time. (Adding 40 percent more time to your estimate is a good place to start.)

430. Many chronically late people report enjoying the rush of adrenaline from that last-minute dash. In fact, it has been reported that people can actually become addicted to that feeling. If that seems like it might be the case for you, then try substituting something else that will give you the same feeling. Maybe the rush of adrenaline from a fifteen-minute run on your treadmill will garner the same result. (But make sure you leave enough time to squeeze it in and not be late!)

431. A feeling of superiority can be the driving force for some chronically late people since they feel so good about telling everyone how much they were able to cram in. They will rattle off a long list of things they accomplished and people will look at them with a sense of awe. But a person can only run on empty for so long, and this is a false sense of superiority. Although people may wonder how you do it all, they might also feel alienated since they can't relate.

432. Rebelling against rules and structure can cause chronic lateness. But the attitude of "I don't want to" or "you can't make me" won't get you too far. (Remember that if you have small children, they learn by example. Years from now they may also have to read this book, or you can spare them by working with a schedule that suits your style and feels doable.)

433. Poor estimations can also account for running late. If you guess it takes you twenty minutes to run an errand when in fact it takes double that amount of time, then it is no wonder you always get home later than predicted on the days when you run that errand. The simple fix is to time yourself the next time, and go by the real time estimate from then on.

434. Most chronically late people are actually optimists at heart. People with a positive attitude will feel more capable and more able to cram lots of stuff into a short period of time. As a result of overestimating, they run late.

435. Contrary to popular belief, most chronically late people are not looking for more attention by making a grand entrance at an event. Usually it just happens, but there are things you can do about it.

436. Sometimes a lack of self-discipline can be the root cause. If you tend to be more lax with schedules, lists, and calendars, don't fear—you won't have to conform to a strict regimen; there is plenty of middle ground.

437. Take comfort in the fact that you simply think of time differently than the average person; this is not good or bad, just different. That fact can be helpful when you find yourself comparing your style to others and criticizing yourself. (Which, by the way, you should stop doing.)

438. Find out how long it actually takes you to do routine tasks. You might think it takes you twenty minutes to shower and dress, but in reality, your routine requires an hour. This is important information and will help keep you from running behind.

439. Instead of setting your clocks ahead, which rarely works for anyone, simply *plan* to be fifteen minutes *early*. When you have plans to meet for dinner at 6:30, set it in your head as 6:15.

440. Locate misplaced items early so you are not stressed out at the last minute, trying to find the cooler you promised to bring to the picnic, for example.

441. Prevent emergencies by preparing early. For example, fill your gas tank when it is only half empty; that way you won't ever be caught realizing that you have little or no gas the moment before you need to leave.

442. Stop over-committing yourself. You must have realistic plans for your day; there are only twenty-four hours, after all. The great thing about under-committing your day is that if you are done with your list, you'll have free time to work on the next day's list or simply enjoy the feeling of being ahead.

443. Eliminate the temptation to procrastinate by finding someone who can support you and hold you accountable. If you know that you tend to view a deadline as more of a starting point than an end goal, try working with someone who can keep you on track.

444. You may find completing long-term projects to be a challenge. Between time management and procrastination issues, along with planning and organization challenges, long-term projects work best if you can team up with others. Break the task up into small parts and ask for your progress to be reviewed often by someone else involved. More often we will get things done when we know others have an expectation of us.

445. Don't allow paperwork to become unmanageable. Focusing on paperwork all at once can be an overwhelming task, so deal with it as you go. Get help from someone if you have a backlog of paperwork to catch up on.

HAVE MORE TIME TODAY!

1. Team up with your spouse to come up with a way to gently remind each other about time issues.
2. When you have to say yes to a project, accept it with grace, but set clear terms for the next time.
3. Choose one way that will work for you to overcome your lateness challenge and put it into action this week.

TRY THIS:

Set all your clocks to the correct time and place a clock in your bathroom if you don't already have one there.

REPEAT AFTER ME:

"I am successfully managing my time."

Part Nine:

Just Do It!

Are you a world-class procrastinator in gold-medal contention at the Procrastination Olympics? Oh wait, you couldn't be since you'd still be filling out the paperwork...where is that paperwork? Do you ever wonder why you have such a knack for putting things off until they are either a crisis or they are no longer relevant? Although this is not a psychology book, I do have some ways to deal with the tasks that seem worse than going to the dentist.

25.

Procrastination and Procrastination Personalities

446. Try doing your least favorite task first thing in the day. Then everything else for the rest of the day is easier, and you won't have the unpleasant task hanging over your head.

447. Plan on giving yourself a reward for a job well-done. This can be anything you choose. As a treat, you might grab a cup of your favorite beverage, watch a movie, or get your nails done.

448. Hold off on the fun stuff until your unpleasant task is out of the way. Your reward does not have to be something out of the ordinary. It can be something you'd normally do, but just *hold off* doing it until you accomplish the task you've been procrastinating about.

449. Going public by telling others what you plan to accomplish is a great way to hold yourself accountable. Since you won't want to risk being embarrassed by not doing what you say you will do, this is a great way to be sure you get the task done.

450. Find a buddy to help you through. Sometimes we just need a little encouragement, support, or someone to hold us accountable. Locate someone who can be your support or who can help you complete the task.

451. Wrap the task around an already existing habit. Let's say you like to watch a certain television program every Monday at 9:00 p.m. You can plan on doing the task right before your show comes on, so that by the time your program starts your task is done. Watching the program is like your reward, and you're more likely to remember and do the task since it's tied to something you are already guaranteed to remember.

452. Sometimes simply focusing on the feeling of being done is enough to help you overcome the procrastination and just get the task over with. When you can imagine how it will feel to be done with the task that has been weighing on you, that can often outweigh the uncomfortable feeling of getting started.

453. Break up large, overwhelming tasks into smaller, more doable portions. It's like the answer to the old question, "How do you eat an elephant?": One bite at a time. By breaking up the task into manageable parts that you can do quickly and more easily, you are less likely to be overwhelmed by the task.

454. If you like to start off slowly and successfully, then you might find tackling a small and easy task first is the best way for you to get rolling. Pick something doable and finish it. This can give you the confidence to then conquer larger, more complex tasks.

455. Keep restarting. Just like anything, when you start and then falter, simply restart and keep going.

456. Keep in mind that getting started is the hardest part. Once you get started, the rest is easy. So just do something to break the ice, and the momentum will build.

457. Recognize that the anxiety about doing the task may be worse than actually doing the task itself. Unpleasant tasks rarely turn out to be as bad as you imagine they will be; often, we envision the task to be so horrible that once it is done, we wonder what all the fuss was about.

458. Do more research. Sometimes we put off doing something because we are not sure what to do. Do some more research to find out what your next step should be. Keep in mind that research counts towards doing the task, so you are no longer putting it off.

459. Ask yourself: What is the one thing I most want to avoid doing today? Then take that answer and identify why. If the task is important, do it anyway; if not, cross it off your list or delegate it.

460. Stop and ask yourself if the task really needs to be done, and if so, if it needs to be done by *you*. Sometimes the task is no longer necessary, or we can delegate it to someone else.

461. Make a decision and move on; you can always make a change later if you need to. Don't get caught up in an inability to make a choice.

462. Sometimes we put something off out of fear of the outcome. Ask yourself, "What is the worst thing that can happen?" Most of the time the answer is something you can live with. Once you know nothing traumatic is going to happen, you can dive in and tackle the task, without fear holding you back.

463. Give a deadline to the entire task, even if you have to create one. For example, if you have been putting off restaining the deck, then send out party invitations to hold a BBQ on the deck. Now you have a deadline since you'll want the deck to be restained by the party!

464. See if someone has done the task before you. If so, use their template to help you start.

465. Stop multitasking. When you divide your attention between multiple tasks, you waste time, since you can't focus as well and the task takes longer. Also, you are less likely to remember things because you are not focusing fully. Instead, give each task 100 percent of your attention, complete it, and then move on.

466. How much time do you find yourself wasting as you deliberate about your options? Analysis paralysis is the term used to describe someone who overthinks choices. That can lead to lots of wasted time. Decide on one of the choices and move forward. You can always change your mind later.

467. Planning is usually easier than just buckling down and getting started. Sometimes we can think, research, plan, and prepare to our detriment since many times enough planning to get started is all that is needed; over planning is a time waster.

468. Worrying is a huge time waster. Asking yourself "what if" questions about things that will probably never come to pass can drain your energy, keep you up at night, have you thinking of solutions, and simply take a toll on you. If you know you have a pattern of worrying, try writing down the next thing you find yourself worrying about and then see if it happens. Most times it won't, and when you see that on paper, it can be easier to change your worry habit.

469. Call a time-out! Sometimes just giving yourself a time-out from everything else around can help you focus on what's in front of you. Set a timer for eighteen minutes, and do the task at hand without surfing the Web, calling friends on the phone, reading, walking around, or anything else—simply work with blinders on until the buzzer sounds.

470. Just do it. Sign up for that class, make that phone call; whatever it is, just do it. Amazingly, once you do, the time finds itself. Take action today. Stop coming up with excuses about how you don't have time. Either you want to do it and you'll make the time—or not.

471. The Perfectionist: This perfectionist procrastination personality is often mistaken for something else, since most people tend to assume that a perfectionist would not allow things to go undone; however, that is not true. Perfectionists have one of the most challenging personalities since they set unrealistically high standards for themselves and have such lofty, unattainable goals that they can never meet their own expectations for themselves. **Solution:** Stop focusing on what you think you should do, and start focusing on what you can realistically accomplish. Then practice setting your standards at good (an attainable level), not perfect (impossible).

472. **Indecisive:** People who have trouble deciding often lack confidence in their ability to make a correct choice. By not taking action, they are forced to live with the consequences, which just reinforces their feeling that they can't make the right choices. **Solution:** Break down the task to the smallest choice that needs to made, then make a decision and act on it. Ask yourself, "What's next?," and take action. You'll quickly see that you are capable, and even if you make a not-so-great choice, you can make a change.

473. **The Defier:** The Defier's favorite phrase is "You can't make me." And while it may be true that you cannot be forced, you're only hurting yourself. The worst part of this is that to avoid confrontations, Defiers might make a commitment halfheartedly and then never follow through on it, disappointing people along the way. **Solution:** See the choices you do have, and choose to take action before someone can ask or force you to take one you'd rather not.

474.

Detail-Challenged: People with detail-challenged personalities are often accused of not caring, when, in fact, they do care—up to a point. When it comes to making decisions about miniscule issues, however, they tend to step off projects. **Solution:** Whenever you can, delegate the details. If delegating is not an option, then simply plow through it knowing that the sooner you deal with the details of this project, the sooner you can get to the big picture on a new project.

475.

The Surfer: If you tend to have the attitude that things will get done "when they get done," then you might be considered a Surfer or coaster. The challenge with this thought pattern is that you can end up working against yourself, allowing your whims to carry you one way and then another. You'll end up doing things over and not progressing toward your goals. Although that laid-back attitude has its place, it shouldn't be your everyday mindset. **Solution:** Choose one or two important goals to work toward while reserving enough space in your calendar to not be ruled by lists, time, or schedules. That balance will allow you to get where you want to go without feeling tremendous amounts of pressure, and the unscheduled blocks of time will energize you enough to get through the more rigid times.

476. Adrenaline Junkie: The surge of adrenaline can be addicting, not to mention all the adoration you get from your fans when you swoop in at the last minute and play the hero. But you can't run on adrenaline alone; the effects on your body and life are far-reaching. **Solution:** Create other challenges as a way of competing against yourself, which can be just as rewarding. Set a timer for thirty minutes, and see how much you can accomplish before the bell rings.

477. I'll get to it later: Or I'll get right back to it or I'll just put it here for now... **Solution:** Get that do-it-now mentality by using the two-minute rule: if you can do a task in two minutes or less, do it right that moment. Instead of putting things off, recognize that you will have no more time later than you do right now. Plus, things always take less time in the moment; get it done now, since later rarely comes.

478. People Pleaser:

People Pleaser: People pleasers don't seem like procrastinators since they are always doing something, but just under the surface, they are holding things together by a very thin thread. Often people pleasers are so overwhelmed—a fact they keep hidden from others—that they lose track of what needs to be done and have to work inefficiently to try to catch up. They have trouble saying no, and they often volunteer themselves for more than they can handle. **Solution:** Hang up your Superman cape or your Wonder Woman lasso immediately. Understand that your need to look so capable in other people's eyes and to continually be praised for your hard work is a desire you can fill in other ways without running yourself ragged. Starting today, practice saying "no" gracefully and stop volunteering to take on more work. In fact, you might even reconsider a commitment and offer to help find your replacement.

26.

Common Myths and Frequent Objections

479. **Myth 1:** You can control time. **The Truth:** It is impossible to manage time. The only thing you can control is how you manage yourself.

480. **Myth 2:** You can get all caught up. **The Truth:** There will always be more to do. Plus, you'd never want to be completely caught up because then you'd be left without anything to do!

481. **Myth 3:** You should do it all yourself. **The Truth:** You shouldn't, and you can't. In fact, it is selfish to insist on doing it all yourself; you take all the credit and never allow others to advance their skills. And whenever you are not able to come through, you put others in a difficult position since they have to fix the problem themselves.

482. **Myth 4:** You can get back to it later. **The Truth:** If you walk away from something without finishing it, there is rarely time to go back later to finish it. Also, it will take longer since you will most likely have forgotten where you left off.

483. **Myth 5:** Your life is out of your control. **The Truth:** You have full control over how you use your time. You may need to make changes or reorganize your priorities, but each day you are in control of how you spend those twenty-four hours.

484. **Myth 6:** If you stop, you'll get farther behind. **The Truth:** Sometimes you need to put the brakes on the hamster wheel and allow yourself time to regroup before you can move in the right direction.

485. Myth 7: It will never work for you. The Truth: Although everyone has different time-management challenges and there is no cookie-cutter solution, there is a system that will work for you, and it takes less time to figure it out then you might think.

486. Myth 8: This is just a phase that will pass. The Truth: Life is made up of phases strung together, so at any given time you are in the midst of a phase. By the time you wait for it to pass, you'll be in the middle of another one.

487. Objection 1: I've tried before, and time management will not work for me. The Reality: If you tried before and it didn't work as you expected, you probably didn't hit on the plan that was right for you. People have different styles, so no single solution works for everyone. Try another solution; a little trial and error will pay off in the long run.

488. Objection 2: I gave it a week, and nothing changed. The Reality: Did you know that it takes twenty-one days to create a new habit and to break an old pattern? You have to try a new idea for at least that long before you can evaluate its effectiveness.

489. Objection 3: I've already tried every-thing. **The Reality:** It is most unlikely that you have tried *everything*; you just might feel like that if you haven't experienced lots of success. Pick a new idea that feels more like a good fit, and give it another shot.

490. Objection 4: It's not that bad; I can handle the stress. **The Reality:** Sure you may be able to handle it, but you don't have to be this stressed-out all the time. Why settle for just getting by when you can enjoy life instead?

491. Objection 5: This is just how my life is now. **The Reality:** While it is true that we may find ourselves busier during certain times in our lives, you don't have to allow it to become a permanent situation. Moving, having a baby, going back to school, and facing a deadline on the job are just a few examples of these stress-ful times, but with a plan to manage your time, you can regain control quickly.

492. Objection 6: I get more done when I am under pressure and working towards a deadline. **The Reality:** That's debatable. It might just feel like you're getting more done since it is so much more overwhelming. And even if it is true, imagine all you could get done if you had more time!

493. Objection 7: I don't do lists. **The Reality:** You don't have to! Some people simply don't work well with a traditional list. There are variations, and you just have to find the one that will better suit your personality.

494. Objection 8: There is nothing I can do. It is other people's fault and out of my control. **The Reality:** While it is true that other people's personalities, styles, and deadlines may infringe on your time, you *do* have control. You can control your response and how you let these outside forces affect you. It's simply a matter of figuring out your options and acting on them.

495. Objection 9: I'm already set in my ways. **The Reality:** Even the most regimented people can find room for a little flexibility if the new idea suits them and makes a positive difference. Pick something and try it out. You will be pleasantly surprised.

496. **Objection 10:** I'm just disorganized; there is no hope. **The Reality:** This is so not true. There is always hope! Start small and take little steps. You have the power to wow yourself. Clutter and time management are related on some levels, but in other areas they are completely unrelated. Choose an area of time management that is unrelated to clutter and start there.

27.

Interruptions, Distractions, and a Clear Head

497. Sometimes interruptions are unavoidable. When that is the case, jot a quick note to remind yourself where you left off. That way, when you are able to get back to the task, you can pick it up more quickly.

498. Avoid time-wasting interruptions and distractions by eliminating the ones you can. Turn off the television and shut off the ringer on the phone for a limited period of time while you work on that one task.

499. Another way to shut out interruptions and distractions is to shut the door of the room where you are working; it can be just for a short period of time while you get through the task. This can be really helpful when completing a fun task, such as wrapping gifts, to avoid others wanting to "help."

500. Hang a "please do not disturb" sign. This may sound odd at first, but after you try this, you'll be hooked. Post a note on a closed door to alert anyone who is thinking of interrupting you that you do not wish to be disturbed for five, ten, twenty minutes, or whatever you need. (It works best if you give a specific ending time so everyone knows when they can expect you to be done. Also, give clear instructions on what is important enough to be interrupted for, like blood or smoke.)

501. Clear the workspace. This is a huge timesaver. When you are surrounded by open projects, notes, ideas, and clutter, you can't focus 100 percent on the task at hand.

502. Open only one project at a time. You may have lots of projects you want to accomplish, but you should only take out the pieces for one at a time. For example, instead of trying to pay the bills near a pile of unfolded laundry, leave the laundry in the basket, so you can focus on paying the bills first without becoming distracted by the laundry.

503. Mental clutter makes you feel like you have less time than you actually do. Plus, you complete tasks more slowly since you are bogged down. Eliminate as much mental clutter as possible. Usually, capturing all the thoughts, items, and ideas floating around in your head and putting them on paper is a good place to start.

504. Stop wasting time looking for notes that you wrote yourself on scraps of paper. Instead, send yourself an email or call your own voice mail or answering machine, and leave yourself a message.

505. Need to remember to take something with you when you leave the house? Place your car keys, purse, or wallet with that item, and you'll be much more likely to remember to take it with you. For example, need to take the casserole to the dinner party? Put the keys in the refrigerator next to the dish.

506. If the item you need to remember to take is nonperishable, take it out and place it in the car when you are thinking about it, so you won't leave without it. Walking out of the house without everything you need costs you time if you stop to buy another of the item or have to go back to get it.

507. If it helps, carry a voice recorder. This allows you to record lists of things to do and thoughts and ideas. And because you don't have to use your hands, you can record while driving or walking.

508. Write it down. Once you write it down, it is off your mind, and a less cluttered mind is a good thing.

509. Set a timer to help you keep track of time. You can do it to remind yourself to take a cake out of the oven, switch tasks, leave for an appointment, or make a call.

510. Sticky notes can help keep you on task and spare you from wasting valuable time. For example, post a sticky note on the computer mouse to remind you not to surf until you finish another task. (Warning: Too many sticky notes is a time-waster. Don't overdo the sticky notes!)

511. A mini whiteboard hung on the door through which you enter and leave your home most often can be helpful for last-minute reminders about what to bring with you. This will save you time so you don't walk out without something you need.

512.

Creating routines helps you save time since you don't have to rethink how to handle certain tasks each time you need to do them. For example, if you are always spending time looking for your keys, you can create a new routine where you always place the keys on a single designated hook. That one simple hook can save you many minutes per day. Routines make life easier.

HAVE MORE TIME TODAY!

1. Pick one way of overcoming procrastination that will best suit you and implement it starting today. Don't put it off. Try it today!
2. See if any of the frequent objections sound like something you've said. If so, resolve yourself to the fact that you are embarking on a new path, and you won't be tied down to old patterns of thinking.
3. Choose a strategy for dealing with interruptions, like writing a note to yourself so you know where you left off.

TRY THIS:

Break tasks up into small parts, and do the first small part; then ask yourself, "What's next?" Do that, and before you know it, the entire task will be done!

REPEAT AFTER ME:

"What can I take action on today?"

Part Ten:

Pets and Hobbies

It can be difficult to find time for the things we love to do like gardening, taking long walks with our pets, or attending yoga classes. If you struggle to add the fun stuff into your life because you are too busy just getting through the day, here are some solutions that will have you getting back to enjoyable things in no time.

28.

Gardening and Pets

513. Choose low-maintenance perennial flowers and evergreen plants as this will save you time replanting.

514. Do research before you buy so you can pick out the correct types of plants and flowers for the space you have. No sense spending time planting and then having to replant if those plants or flowers don't work in the spot. (Good bets are daylilies for sunny spots or hostas and impatiens for shady areas.)

515. Stop running back and forth from the garden to the garage by placing a decorative mailbox in the garden to store those much-needed tools like a trowel, twine, scissors, pruning sheers, and whatever else you find yourself reaching for.

516. Setting up a shed, even a small one, can prevent extra trips to and from the garage for commonly used items. Place the shed near the garden so that items can be stored in a more convenient location. A bonus will be more free space in your garage.

517. To easily tote the tools and supplies you need into the garden, put them all into a garbage can on wheels and wheel them into the garden.

518. Store the plant-care tags in a three-ring binder filled with clear plastic sheet protectors for easy reference in the future.

519. Place unused seed packets in a clear plastic watertight box. Label the box, and place the packets inside for safekeeping. You might also consider keeping a permanent marker in the box so you can easily label and date the seed packets before you store them. Dating the seeds is useful since it can be easy to forget how old they are.

520. The next time you go to fertilize your plants, measure out fertilizer into one-time-use ziplock baggies for future use. By filling each baggie with enough fertilizer for one watering, you can avoid having to measure each time you need to fertilize.

521. Watering the garden can take a lot of time out of your day. Using a soaker hose can free you up. You can take one of your everyday garden hoses and put puncture holes in it to create your own homemade soaker hose.

522. Automate your watering routine by placing the soaker hose or sprinkler on an automatic timer. The timer simply screws on between the hose and the spigot.

523. If you need to water two areas of the lawn, run two hoses from the same spigot by adding a simple T and water two areas at once.

524. Adding mulch or a plastic sheet to line the garden area can prevent weed growth and keep you from having to spend time weeding.

525. Do pruning jobs faster by using a ratcheting pruner. These ratcheting tools allow you to cut through branches more quickly and with less effort. Black and Decker sells an alligator pruner that does a great job.

526. Use the right glove for the right job. Instead of wasting time trying to avoid thorns when cutting roses or picking up pricker branches, try puncture-proof gloves.

527. An automatic waterer for indoor plants can save you time since you won't have to pull out the watering can so often. Plug the automatic drip into a plastic soda bottle, and insert it into the potted plant. The water will drip out and continuously water the plant.

528. Sticking a moisture meter into the soil can help you determine when the plant is in need of watering. An audible one like the Frog Doctor will alert you by signaling with a tone so you don't even have to remember to check the meter!

529. Save time searching for your pet's favorite toys by giving them homes. If you tend to use toys in more than one room, then make a home for toys in each room so you do not end up running from room to room when you need to clean up.

530. Keep your pet leashes nearest the door you use most often. To avoid wasting time untangling the leashes, consider purchasing the retractable type. Always put the leashes back in the same spot so you can find them again quickly. If you need to take cleanup bags out with you, leave those with the leashes as well.

531. Pack a travel bag for those days when you are going to take your dog to the dog park or for a long walk or car ride and need to have water and a snack on hand. Keep nonperishable items in the bag, like a toy and a water dish, and just before leaving you can grab a bottle of water.

532. For pet cages that need to be cleaned, create a cleaning caddy with the commonly used cleaning items, like rags and rubber gloves. Then you can grab all the supplies easily instead of hunting down each item every time you need it.

533. Organize your pet's paperwork, especially the veterinarian's contact information and the pet's records, someplace you can access it quickly in the event of an emergency. A single brightly colored envelope stored on a bookshelf is one way to keep it handy. Sometimes trying to find papers in a filing cabinet takes too much time.

534. Opt for easy-to-use storage containers for things like food pellets and cedar bedding chips. Choose storage containers that close tightly and toss a scoop inside to use. Also be sure to label the outside of the container so you know what is inside at a glance.

535. Store all medication for your pet in a completely different location from all the other medication in the house. You'd never want to confuse them with medications meant for humans.

536. Write your veterinarian's number on a piece of paper along with emergency contact numbers, like the twenty-four-hour animal hospital, and hang the paper near the phone so it is handy in case you ever need to use it. During a crisis, you won't have time to waste looking for phone numbers and contact information.

537. Automate whatever you can. The less time you have to spend on maintenance, the more time you'll have to do other things. Try using a water dish that allows you to screw on a two-liter soda bottle filled with water so you'll have to refill the bowl less often.

538. If you have a fish tank, add a vacation timer to the outlet where you plug in the light so it will turn on and off automatically at the times of the day you set it for. That way you can cross one thing off your daily to-do list.

539. If you have indoor cats, try an auto-scooping cat litter box. The automatic raking system pulls the waste into a bag which means you spend less time scooping out litter boxes. (Simply lining the cat litter box saves time since you won't have to wash it clean every time.)

540. To clean pet fur from chairs and couches, use a lint roller. Using a lint roller on a long handle allows you to roll the floors as well, since sometimes a vacuum simply blows the hair around, meaning you have to spend more time to clean it up.

541. Taking your pet to see the veterinarian for regular healthy pet checkups means that many time-consuming and expensive emergencies can be averted.

29.

Crafting/ Sewing

542. Even if you don't have a designated "craft room," try adding a slimline floor-to-ceiling bookshelf that you can designate as your craft area. If little fingers will pull items off the lower shelves, then consider using a computer armoire as your crafting area. With the slide-out shelf, you'll have added workspace, and there are cubbies in which to organize your supplies. Best of all, it shuts and can lock if you need it to.

543. Put a project in a carry tote even if you only plan to carry it around the house. You'll spend less time looking for all the supplies. That means the time you have to craft can be spent crafting and not hunting down what you need to get started.

544. An over-the-door clear plastic shoe holder can be a perfect spot to store notions and tools. The clear, plastic pockets allow you to see what you have and get to it easily whenever you need it.

545. Store like items together; that way you can see what you already own more easily and you won't waste time rebuying things. If you have trouble deciding what to store together, think of how a store is set up. If you'd find the items in an aisle together, then store them at home together.

546. A simple way to store patterns and projects in progress is to slip everything into a one-gallon ziplock baggie. With just one glance you can easily tell which project is which, and you'll have all the pieces to go along with it on hand.

547. Clearly label everything! Labels make things easy to locate, and they speed up cleaning since you know right where to toss everything.

548. Another way to save time with cleanup, or when trying to locate something you dropped (like a button), is to opt for a non-carpeted surface. Carpet in your crafting room creates more work, so consider working on a wood, linoleum, or tile surface. Not only is it easier to clean up, but your chair will roll more smoothly, meaning you can zip around from spot to spot while working.

549. Live by the old adage: measure twice and cut once. You'll make fewer mistakes and save lots of time.

550. Stop rereading magazines and books to locate that one project you thought would be great. Instead, when you see something you like, pop a sticky note on the page and leave a little tab so you can write a description of what is on the page. Then when you are looking for something you saw, you can read the tabs to find it easily.

30.

You Might Already Be Exercising

551. Use your lunchtime at home or at the office to take a walk.

552. Play with your children or pets while exercising. Instead of sitting and watching them, get involved in the action and toss a ball, hula-hoop, or do anything else that gets you up and moving.

553. As you do routine chores, you can blend in some exercising. For example, when putting the groceries away, use both hands to carry and lift, or when vacuuming, instead of bending at the waist, do deep knee bends when vacuuming under the tables and chairs.

554. Move your exercise machine to be near the washing machine. Then when you put in a load of laundry, stay there and exercise.

555. Choose the stairs at work or in the mall, and forgo the elevator.

556. Park in one of the farthest spots from the entrance and walk.

557. Choose combination exercises where you work more than one muscle group at a time so you can get your workout done faster.

558. Preassemble an exercise kit with everything you need to work out. No more wasting time running around looking for equipment, towels, headphones, or water bottles. That means more time to spend exercising and less time to talk yourself out of wanting to do the work.

559. Keep a stash of exercise clothing on hand, so you won't have to spend time sifting through your closet or dresser drawers.

560. If you have been having a hard time trying to fit exercising into your schedule, or you've been waiting to exercise in your spare time, the best solution is to schedule it. Make an appointment with yourself to do it, and you will be more likely to follow through. Try exercising with a friend whom you would normally socialize with; instead of going out, have them come over and work out as a team.

561. Organize a walking book group. Talk about the book as you walk. Multitasking at its best!

562. Another way to get two things done at once is to watch your favorite television show, read, or listen to a book on tape while doing your exercise routine. Doing both at the same time frees up thirty to sixty minutes of your time later. Plus, you are more apt to do it since you have a routine and also might enjoy it more.

563. Walk your children to school. This is a great timesaver since you can get your exercise in and catch up with what's been going on with them. You can also opt to walk back home with another parent so you can socialize while exercising.

HAVE MORE TIME TODAY!

1. If you garden or have a pet, move one supply item to a more convenient location.
2. Give away one project you started and never completed so someone else can finish it. You will have more time for a new project that you do enjoy.
3. Take a look at your day, and find an easy way to add just a little more physical activity to it, like parking farther away in the parking lot.

TRY THIS:

Find a friend who is also looking to add more enjoyable things to her week, and sign up together for something fun. It can be a one-night class or a decision to walk together one morning a week.

REPEAT AFTER ME:

"I deserve to make time in my day for things that I enjoy."

Part Eleven:

I Was Promised a Paperless Society

Picture this: Company is due to arrive in fifteen minutes, and the doorbell rings—they're early! You fly into super mode, and with a laundry basket or paper bag in hand, you scoop up piles of papers and mail from countertops and tables. You then dump it all in a closet, the garage, or the basement with every intention of getting to it later...but later never comes. If you too have made one (or more) of these scoop-and-dump bags, baskets, or boxes, you are not the only one. Paper is a huge issue and takes so much time to deal with. With all the decisions you have to make, all the junk mail you have to destroy, and all the demands on your time, it's no wonder we put off dealing with the piles of paper. But there is an easier way to sort through the piles and to save more time.

31.

Mail and Often-Referenced Pending Paper

564. Stop wasting time shredding the preapproved credit card offers sent to you by various banks. Instead, remove yourself from the mailing lists for free through the Federal Trade Commission. Go to www.optout prescreen.com or dial 1-888-567-8688.

565. Reduce the amount of junk mail you deal with by requesting your name be removed from the junk mail mailing lists. Send a signed and dated letter to Direct Marketing Association, Junk Mail Service, P.O. Box 643, Carmel, NY 15012.

566. When you send your letter to the Direct Marketing Association, you *must* include each and every way that junk mail comes addressed to you. Sometimes they may use your initials or spell your name incorrectly, and so on. You have to include those versions of your name in the letter you send since the data entry person will remove you from the database based on the information you provide. To make this easier, for the next month or two, clip the address part off each piece of junk mail and put it in an envelope. Then staple the addresses to the signed letter and send it off. (You can save even more time by printing off the letter from www.jamienovak.com. All you have to do is fill in the blanks and mail it.)

567. Stop reading junk mail; this is a huge time-waster. If you know it's junk, toss it immediately. If you are unsure, open it, glance at it, and if it is junk, toss it. We already know that there are no get-rich-quick schemes that work.

568. To speed up the mail-opening process, invest in a battery-operated letter opener; it will cost less than most lunches and save lots of time.

569. Do you spend a lot of time sorting though charitable donation requests? Do you wonder how the organization got your name if you never donated to them directly? Well, most charities make a significant amount of their money by selling their mailing lists. So before you donate to another organization, take a moment to check out the charity's rating. Go to www.charitywatch.org or the Better Business Bureau website (www.bbb.org) and click charity ratings.

570. Whenever you fill out a product registration form or provide your contact information on any paper, check the "opt out," box, indicating that you do not wish to have your name sold to other mailing lists. The same is true whenever you give your phone number at a checkout register; the company can use a reverse lookup function to find your address in order to solicit you.

571. Sorting your papers is a simple way to save time. Instead of piling a bunch of unrelated papers into one pile, try keeping like papers together. This will save you time when you need to retrieve a paper.

572. Put the papers in the right place the first time and stop wasting time moving papers from spot to spot. For example, instead of placing the newspaper on the kitchen chair when you are done reading it, then moving it to the countertop, and finally putting it on the recycling stack in the garage, take the extra steps to the recycling in the garage and put it there to begin with. (If you notice papers are being left out consistently, try making the bin more convenient. If the recycling in the garage is not easy to reach, make a mini recycling station someplace more convenient.)

573. Stand the papers up—they are much easier to find when vertical. Your new rule is that all papers stand on end rather than laying down horizontally. Not only are they easier to find that way, but they also take up much less space.

574. Color-coded folders can save time, since you will be able to visually connect the papers inside the folder with the color of the folder. At a glance you'll know that take-out menus are in the red folder and bills to be paid are in the green folder. This translates to less time searching for papers.

575. Set up a system for the mail that comes for other people in the house. Once you know where to put their mail and how much to let accumulate before you sort it for them, you can save valuable time.

576. If you find that you waste time looking through piles of paper that you will never really read, stop bringing paper into your home in the first place. Do not bring home the minutes to your organization's meeting, multiple copies of the school newsletter, or the brochure from the bank.

NO-FAIL PAPER SOLUTION

This is a foolproof system for dealing with all the pending papers in your life. This is the exact one I've used for years, and the one I set my clients up with. This is the real McCoy; don't be fooled by imitations.

This system is great for dealing with all the pending papers in your life. You know, the ones that sit in a pile on your tables and countertops waiting for you to do something with them. The trick is to keep them out and accessible without having them scattered every which way from Tuesday. How are you going to do this? By using a desktop file box. This desktop box will most likely sit on the kitchen countertop since you want to have the papers on hand.

This type of box has no lid and accommodates about twenty letter-size hanging folders. The boxes come in a wide variety of styles and colors and are available at office stores and most home goods stores. They range in price, but most are under twenty dollars. You'll want to find one that blends with your décor, since it will be sitting out.

Here's what you're going to need to whip your paper piles into shape:

- A desktop file box
- Set of hanging folders (any color)
- Pad of 2" x 2" sticky notes
- Pen
- Calendar

To deal with any backlog of papers that may be sitting around:

1. Set your kitchen timer for eighteen minutes and jump in. You won't finish the job, but that is enough time to make a serious dent.

2. Gather up all your pending paperwork from the countertops and tables.

3. Sit down and separate the paperwork into piles of like items, for example: all the bills, all the items to read, photos, coupons, receipts, and so on.

4. As you sort into piles, toss the no-brainer stuff, like expired coupons. But *do not* get caught in decision-making about the papers. This is not the time to decide whether to keep it or toss it. It is also not the time to think about whether to renew that magazine subscription or if you do or do not want to go to the party you've been invited to. Instead, toss the invitation in the invitations pile and move on.

5. Once you have the large pile sorted into

smaller piles with specific categories, you are almost done.

6. Next, grab a hanging folder and put all similar papers in the file.

7. Use a sticky note to label the file. Stick the sticky part of the note to the file, and leave the rest of the note sticking up as the label. There are no perfect label names, just write something that will help you remember what is inside. "Important," "pending," "this week," and "urgent" are not the best choices, since so many of the papers potentially fall in those categories. Instead use names like, "sports schedules," "social invitations," "scouts," and so on. A more complete list is below.

8. The final step in the process is to note anything that needs your attention on the calendar. Since you won't want to sift through each file every day to see what needs your attention, you'll want to be prompted. Let's say, for example, that you need to sign your child up for swim lessons by the twentieth of the month. On the calendar, write in a box about a week earlier "swim sign-up paper in swim folder." When you look at your calendar that day you'll be reminded not only to sign up, but where the paper is. And since it will be about a week before the deadline, there will not be a last-minute rush.

Here is an example of how a paper might flow through your new system.

The mail comes in today and you receive a community school brochure that you'd like to flip through. You may or may not register for a class; you need to read the brochure first. Open the brochure to the registration page to see what the registration deadline is. Go to your calendar and write in a note about a week before the deadline to remind yourself to read the brochure that is filed in the community school folder. Then take a sticky note and write "community school" on it. Put the label on the file, put the brochure inside, and tuck it away. When the date rolls around, you will see the note on the calendar reminding you that you need to read the brochure. Start carrying the brochure with you so you can glance at it in your spare time. If nothing catches your eye, then toss the brochure. If you see something you want to register for, either fill out the form and send the check in or, if you have enough time, put it in the bill file to be paid during the next bill-paying session. Write the date of the class on the calendar. Then, place the brochure back in the community school file, since you'll want to have it on hand to refer to the day of the class so you have all the pertinent information. Done!

These files live here a short time; the summer camp file stays only until you register for summer camp or until camp is ended. But no longer. Other files, like bills and receipts, stay, but the contents only stay a little while. That is why you use the sticky notes instead of the plastic tabs. Since the files are temporary, there is no sense in wasting time making file tabs. Although, for the files that are for long-term categories, like "bills" and "receipts," you may choose to use the tabs, since the sticky notes will eventually fall off.

Here are some examples of what belongs in which basic folder:

- Household: warranties and instruction manuals
- To Read: magazine articles, newsletters
- Receipts: receipts from the current month
- Recipes
- Pay Stubs: pay stubs or direct deposit statements
- Travel: brochures, other ideas
- Entertainment: tickets to events and newspaper clippings of upcoming ideas
- Bills: bills to be paid
- To File: select papers that will be moved to a permanent file
- Taxes: items needed for the upcoming tax filing
- Contacts: business cards and scraps of paper with names and numbers
- Photos: to be put into an album
- Family Meeting: topics to be discussed
- baby-sitter: things your baby-sitter needs to know
- Schedules: sports schedules, recycling calendars, event calendars
- Health: kids' medical records, prescriptions, physician referrals
- Directions
- Social Engagements: party invitations, directions to the events
- Restaurants: restaurants you want to try and restaurant reviews
- Coupons: coupons and gift certificates
- Grocery Shopping: sales flyers, shopping list, food store coupons

- Discussion: things to ask your spouse about
- Day Trips: brochures and ideas of day trips to take
- Books to Read: lists of books you'd like to read one day and book reviews
- Movies to See: a list of movies you'd like to see and movie reviews
- Gifts: ideas of gifts to buy for others or a wish list for yourself, pictures clipped from catalogs stapled to the order information
- Instructions: clippings of a craft pattern, decorating a cake, or other directions
- Take-Out Menus: menus for the local restaurants and corresponding coupons
- Banking: deposit and withdrawal receipts, monthly statement to be reconciled
- Clippings: newspaper or magazine clippings that do not fit another category but would be good to refer to at some point
- Online: websites that have been recommended to you or that you would like to check out one day
- Investments: brokerage house statements
- School: lunch tickets, school work in progress, school calendar
- Spiritual: schedules of events
- Memory Box: artwork and other items to be saved in a treasure box
- "Hairstyle Ideas," "Places to Visit," "Landscaping," "PTA," "Cub Scouts," "Bake Sale," "Kitchen Remodel," "Birthday Party," "Halloween Costumes," "Holiday Card Writing," "Getting Organized," and so on
- Give each family member his or her own file

Remember, however, your box will be personalized since every person has different papers. You may have some or all of these categories and others like hairstyles, places to visit, landscaping, and so on. For more on the No-Fail Paper Solution visit www.jamienovak.com.

32.

But What If I Want to Save It?

577. Stop stacking your magazine and newspaper clippings into piles. Finding papers in a pile is very time-consuming. Instead, to save time locating an item you clipped from a magazine, newspaper, or catalog, take a one-inch, three-ring binder and fill it with a bunch of top-loading, clear, plastic sheet protectors. The next time you clip something out, grab your binder and slide it in right away. The sheet protectors are easy to use and even if your item is double-sided you'll be able to read both sides without removing the clipping. Be sure to label the spine of the binders with the contents so you know what is inside each one at a glance. (For a full list of suggested categories and other ways to use the binder visit www.jamienovak.com.)

578. Think before you clip. Most of the information we clip out and hold onto is available somewhere else. Plus, if we don't remember we have it when we need it, then we won't even use it—and all that clipping ends up being a huge waste of time. So unless you have a specific plan for using the information, like clipping day-trip ideas at the start of the summer, you might not need to spend the time.

579. Think before you print. Sometimes it is just as easy or easier to save the information on your computer instead of printing it out and having to find a place to put the paper. Try bookmarking the web page, or copy and paste the item into a new document. Then you can simply save the document in a folder on the computer with a title that clearly identifies the contents.

580. Think before you file. So many of us are spending time filing away papers that we don't even need. Did you know that over 90 percent of what is filed is never referenced again? (Not sure what you need and what you can toss? Visit www.jamienovak.com for a current suggested retention schedule.)

NO-FAIL BINDER SOLUTION

A simple and portable way to keep all your stuff together!

Step One: Decide on the type of binder you're going to create

Step Two: Insert the readily available items into your preassembled binder*

Step Three: Label the binder and use

Step Four: As you locate more items, integrate them into the binder

*Do not wait until you have located all the items to start making the binder. Just get started, and add as you go.

INCLUDED IN YOUR BINDER:

• Lined notebook paper (for jotting down ideas)
• Clear page protectors (no need to hole-punch)
• Zippered pencil pouch (to hold pens and loose items)
• Large tabbed dividers (to categorize your binder)

TYPES OF BINDERS YOU CAN CREATE

Suggested Contents:

Household Manual: Commonly referred to items, playdate phone numbers, class schedules

Driving Directions: directions, maps

To Read: items you've been meaning to read so you can easily take them with you

Travel Ideas: ideas, plans, brochures, prices, travel agencies, online sites

Vacation: what you want to see, packing lists, itineraries

Recipes: clipped recipes sectioned by category

Receipts: receipts placed in sheet protectors and organized by type of charge

School Papers: children's returned tests, half-done homework, and so on

Association: paperwork relating to an organization or group you belong to

Family Members: each person gets one with things like schedules and an address book

Take-Out Menus: restaurant take-out menus (keep a duplicate in your car)

Hobby: instructions, directions, and ideas for your hobby

Warranties and Manuals: warranties, receipts, and manual books stored by category

Remodel: paint chips, business cards, estimates, fabric swatches

New Baby: hospital information, name ideas, doctor information

Moving: utility contact information, mover estimates, to-do lists

Wedding: planning, ideas, contracts, business cards, guest list

Party: location ideas, menu, guest list, business cards

Job Search: resumes, list of contacts, wanted section clippings

Get Organized: ideas, directions, contacts, websites for tips and resources, articles

Financial: what accounts you have, with whom, and their contact information

Bill Paying: creditors, envelopes, stamps, calculator, checkbook

Medical Records: physicians' names, copies of reports, medication list

Reference Clippings: clippings from magazines and newspapers

Health Clippings: relevant magazine and newspaper clippings

Ideas: movies to see, books to read, places to visit, and other lists

Exercise Moves: clippings and ideas for getting fit stored by category

Business Cards: contacts, business cards, and return addresses from envelopes

Greeting Cards: greeting cards sectioned by category

Directions/Instructions: how to do things like craft directions, cake-decorating ideas, etc.

Gardening: plant care tags, lists of what you planted, and the results

33.

Bill-Paying, Filing, and Record-Keeping 101

FINANCES SIMPLIFIED

Take just eighteen minutes to get started. You may not fill all the folders in that time, but you'll have them set up. Going forward, you can fill them as you locate the papers, because each important paper will have a home.

Here's what you'll need to set up your system in eighteen minutes:

- 10–15 hanging folders
- 25+ manila file folders
- Marker

18 uninterrupted minutes

STEP 1: LABEL EACH OF THE HANGING FOLDERS WITH THESE TITLES

- Tax Returns

- Retirement
- Social Security
- Investments
- Bank Accounts
- Household Accounts
- Credit Cards/Loans
- Insurance
- Wills/Trusts
- Children's Accounts

STEP 2: LABEL THE MANILA FILE FOLDERS TO GO INSIDE EACH OF THE HANGING FOLDERS

Tax Returns: 1999, 2000, 2001, 2002, 2003, 2004, 2005, 2006, 2007. Put the tax returns for each year in the corresponding folder. (The files for the upcoming tax years give you room to grow.)

Retirement: One folder for each of the financial institutions that maintains your investments (401K, IRAs, etc.); keep the quarterly and year-end statements.

Social Security: One file folder for each person to hold the statement that comes from the government.

Investments: One file per investment account (not including retirement accounts); examples are mutual funds, CDs, stocks, and brokerage accounts.

Bank Accounts: One file per checking and/or savings account.

Household Accounts: Home title (lease if you rent), home improvements, mortgage.

Credit Cards/Loans: One file per credit card, loan, student loan, and anyone else to whom you owe money.

Insurance: One file per policy—health, life, car, homeowners, renter's long-term care, etc.

Wills/Trusts: One file per will, trust, or living will, along with the lawyer's contact information and instruction on where to find important keys to other important documents.

Children's Accounts: One file folder per minor who has accounts.

That's it. You've done the hard part. Once you set this up in one filing drawer, you will be able to fill in the files as you find the paperwork. Imagine the peace of mind that comes with being able to find these documents when you need them.

581. Save trips to the bank just to deposit your paycheck; opt for direct deposit instead. (When you fill out the direct deposit form, you usually have an option to choose how to deposit the money: all into one account or split between two. If you choose automatic split deposit, this can save you time transferring money from one account to another.

582. Whenever you can, consolidate accounts. For example, move all your insurances to one company; that way you can pay one bill. Often, you'll even get a discount.

583. You can file faster if you set up your filing by month instead of by company. It is much simpler to slip papers and payment stubs into a single file labeled with the month you paid it, rather than to sort them by company. You can save even more time by using a thirteen slot accordion folder, one slot per month, instead of setting up files.

584. Try paying your bills online. If this is a new concept to you, then try it with just one bill. Once you see how simple it is and that your payments are applied correctly, you'll probably want to pay *all* your bills online. Most banks offer free bill-paying service, and it only takes about ten minutes to set up all your accounts.

585. Once you have your bill-paying set up online, you can avoid logging on and paying your bills monthly by prescheduling payments. For routine bills, like utilities that have consistent recurring amounts, you can schedule the checks to be sent on specific days. Then as you open the bills, if for any reason the amount is significantly higher, you can change the amount before the payment is sent, or if the amount is lower, you can leave it alone and have a credit with the company.

586. Pay your bills automatically through your credit cards. You can authorize the companies to deduct their money from your credit card. This is especially nice if you get cash back at the end of the year from the credit card company or earn travel miles. This is *not* a good idea if you know you don't always pay off your balance at the end of every month. When your credit card bill arrives, it is important to look it over to be sure the proper amount was charged, but this still takes less time than writing out bills.

587. Think outside the file. There is no law that requires you to file papers in a traditional filing cabinet. That doesn't work for everybody. Instead, make filing easy. You might find a decorative basket will work for you; keep the basket on a bookshelf and toss the newest paper on top. Use one basket per category—just do not mix categories; it will be too confusing. Then if you ever need to reference a paper, it will already be in date order with the most recent on top.

588. Storing your important papers in a disaster-proof box at home will save you trips to the bank. Only use a bank safety deposit box if you do not need to reference your important papers often. Plus, if for any reason you need them quickly and the bank is closed, you will still have access to them.

TWENTY-TWO THINGS TO PLACE IN DISASTER-PROOF STORAGE:

589. Automobile insurance cards and policies

590. Certificates of birth or death

591. Marriage licenses

592. Car registrations and titles

593. Bank account numbers

594. Deeds and titles

595. Copy of driver's licenses

596. Insurance policies and copies of cards

597. Investment records

598. Mailing list of family and friends

599. Medical history

600. Military records

601. Pin numbers

602. Residency letter (a letter from the state sent to you at current address to prove you reside there)

603. Social security cards

604. Tax records

605. Will/living will or advance directive or durable powers of attorney for health care

606. Photo negatives and one wedding and baby photo

607. Papers or records that prove ownership (such as real estate deeds, automobile titles, and stock and bond certificates)

608. Final legal papers (such as divorce decrees and property settlement papers)

609. Household inventory

610. Any letter that proves an account is paid off in full

HAVE MORE TIME TODAY!

1. Go through your mail when you bring it inside, and make it easier to open by using a battery-operated letter opener.
2. Pick a way to store the papers and clippings you want to keep in a way that will make it easy for you to find them again.
3. Set up a paid bill file system that works for you.

TRY THIS:

Purchase a disaster-proof storage case and, using the list above, find one item a week to place inside. In a few short weeks, your box will be filled and you'll rest easier.

REPEAT AFTER ME:

"I go through my mail when I bring it in; I *do not* put it down."

Part Twelve:

Screen Suckers and Surfing (And I Don't Mean in the Ocean)

How much time per week would you estimate that you spend deleting spam? Well, if you are average, then you are wasting about forty minutes per week! That can add up to anywhere from seven to ten days a year just deleting spam emails. Here's how to get some of that time back.

34.

Email

611. The more emails there are in your inbox, the more time it takes to focus on the important ones. Be sure you have a spam-blocker program installed, and take an extra moment to refine the filters so the most spam can be caught.

612. Set up different email accounts for different purposes. You might think that having a few email accounts would waste time, but in fact, having multiple accounts can save you valuable time. Set up one for friends and family only, one for receipts and statements, one for newsletters and e-zines, one for any organizations or associations you belong to, one for plain and simple junk, and so on; then give the appropriate address out as necessary. For example, some websites require you to register by providing an email address—give them the junk one. That way, when they sell your name and email address to another company, the junk emails they send you will not bog down the more important emails you get from friends and family. You can use your organization email address for your child's school, for example, to email you the minutes from the PTA meeting; if in the future you ever want to read the minutes, you'll have them, but if not, they are not taking up your space and time.

613. If junk emailers already have your friends-and-family email address, try adding an alternate email address and giving it to friends and family only, making sure you check that one daily.

614. Clear out your "sent" email box once a week instead of daily. That way, if an email does not go through, you can copy or cut and paste from the sent version, avoiding a lengthy rewrite.

615. If available, use the preview option when reviewing your email. This feature allows you to read the first few lines of an email without opening the email itself. It's an easy way to catch spam without the risk of opening a virus-infected email. I can assure you that no people overseas have money sitting in an account that they need your help (and your money) to get to, so you can feel confident about skipping those emails.

616. Stop wasting time continuously checking your email. Instead, get in a routine of checking your email one or two times a day. (To make this more successful, turn off your email notification, so you won't be tempted to open your email each time a new message arrives.)

617. Set a timer when reading the email to avoid excessive Internet surfing. The timer ticking down nearby will remind you to focus on the email and not to click on all the links included inside it. It's tempting, but try to avoid it.

618. During the time that you set aside to read emails, instead of just reading them, take the time to actually process them. The difference lies in taking the action required. Reading them is easy; your job is to *do* something with the email. Treat them as if they are pieces of paper—don't let them pile up!

619. Set up folders so you can sort and file the emails within your email program. (Some email programs can be directed to send emails directly into folders so they never hit your inbox. This might be helpful for newsletters you subscribe to or statements and receipts that just need to be saved for reference.)

620. Within your email program there is an option to color-code your incoming emails. Simply put, this means that emails from specific senders will appear in your inbox in color instead of the standard black text; this helps them stand out from the crowd. All you have to do is choose a color to apply to specific email addresses. For example, you could apply the color red to the incoming emails from your boss, or blue to emails from your child's soccer coach. Then, at a glance, you can easily distinguish important emails instead of having to read each subject line.

621. Use caution when color coding your incoming emails. Overdoing the color-coding actually makes it *more* difficult to read your email. Choose to color code only three to five categories of emails.

622. Politely request removal from friends' and family's broadcast email lists—you know the ones: where they blast their entire address list with the joke of the day or a scam warning. If you feel embarrassed to ask, just blame it on me. Let them know you read this book, and I insist you get caught up with your current inbox before receiving "fun" emails—unusual, but it works!

623. If friends and family do not respond to your request to be removed from their broadcast emails, simply provide them with one of the alternate email addresses you set up and plan to check it infrequently.

624. Don't broadcast emails to people in your address book. It takes time to send those emails out, and if you don't always like getting them, you can imagine friends and family feel the same way. Plus, many request that they send it back to you, and you know what that means: even more emails in your inbox.

625. Stop signing up for the joke of the day, your daily horoscope, and other daily emails. You can read them online if you like them that much, but they clog your inbox, and often the email-list owners will sell your email address so you are also bombarded with spam.

626. Unsubscribe from e-zines and e-newsletters you no longer read. It takes a lot less time to unsubscribe once than it does to have to constantly clear your inbox of unwanted email or to get caught up reading them. To determine whether or not you will miss the emails, sign up for a new free email account and have the emails sent there. You can check that email address when you have time, but in the meantime, your main email will be clearer. If you do not find yourself checking the alternate email, then you know those emails are not missed.

627. Thinking of switching email providers but dreading having to notify everyone of your new email address? Use a service that does it for you; www.trueswitch.com allows you to register and then notifies everyone of a change in your email service provider.

628. Whenever you provide your personal information online or sign up for an e-zine, place an online order, or register for something, be sure to read and select the correct "opt out" option. Sometimes, you must check a box to receive additional emails or information, but more often, you must uncheck a box so that they won't automatically follow-up with additional email offers, coupons, newsletters, etc.

629. Don't fall for the marketing ploys meant to make you feel like you'll be missing something if you don't opt to receive newsletters and coupons.

630. Stop entering online contests. They take lots of time to enter, and in the end, they only serve to collect your personal information for companies to sell. If you feel you must enter a particular contest, first check the company out with the Better Business Bureau at www.bbb.org.

631. Recheck the "opt out" box if your first submission fails. If you enter and submit your information online, but encounter an error message that sends you back to the same page, the "opt out" box that you purposely checked (or unchecked) may default back to its original setting. Be sure to recheck it, fix the required information, and resend.

632. If you are required to have multiple website passwords, grab a Rolodex and write the website name and password on the Rolodex cards. Then slide the card into the tab with the letter of the website's name.

633. If you are a Microsoft Office user, don't forget to use the office assistant. Stop wasting time scrolling through the help feature for the answer to your question or trying to figure it out on your own. Instead, type your question into the assistant, and get your answer quickly.

634. Learn the technology of your email account. You'd be surprised what time-saving tips and tricks are available. If you don't know about them or how to use them, you can't take advantage of them. Each email account comes with different options; take a moment to learn yours, and it will be time well spent.

635. Say it in the subject line. When sending messages, be as specific as possible in the subject line as possible. For example, instead of a subject line that reads "meeting changed" type "3pm mtg in conf room A NOT B." This will help you eliminate confusion caused by people not reading emails fully; plus, it saves time for the reader of the email and may help him or her learn to do the same for you.

636. Take a moment and set up a signature line. This is simply the text that you want each email to end with, and setting it up once avoids you having to retype it each and every time you send an email. For example, if you own a home-based business that sells beauty products, you might want to end each email with your name, phone number, website link, and a note that says "Simply Beautiful!" Note: You can have more than one signature line, you just have to go in and select the one you want to use—it's still faster than retyping.

637. Instead of spending time following up with people to be sure they received your emails, you can opt to be notified when an email is delivered and/or read. All you have to do is check the box for the option *prior to* sending the email. (It is not advised to ask for a confirmation on each and every email you send. That would jam up your inbox, so use this option only when necessary.)

638. Use the priority button to designate a sense of urgency to an email that you need the recipient to open immediately. Doing so will get your email the attention it needs. (Do not overuse this option, or you run the risk of others ignoring the priority on future emails since you use it too often.)

639. If you need to send the same information to more than one person, opt for the copy option and send a single email. Using the carbon copy (CC:) option means the people you are addressing the email to *will* be able to see who else is receiving the message. Another option is the blind carbon copy (BCC:); if you use this, the addressees *will not* be able to see who else you copied.

640. Take an extra moment and add new email addresses to the email program's address book. The time it takes to do this now means a huge time-savings in the future. (Choose one standard way of adding people's addresses, either by first or last name. Neither way is particularly preferable, but not having a standard way means you may waste time looking for them under different letters of the alphabet.)

641. Instead of wasting time typing a whole new email when you want to reply to someone, simply click the reply button. This saves their email address in the "to:" line and the original subject line in the subject box.

642. Using the forwarding option is yet another way to save time when emailing. When you want to forward an already-typed message to someone else, simply click the "forward" button, instead of retyping the entire message.

643. Do you need to reply to each person who was copied on the email? Just click the "reply all" button and type one response to the group. (Use caution with this option; you don't want to find yourself typing an unflattering message and sending it to everyone when in fact it was not meant for everyone's eyes!)

35.

Internet

644. Many of us have our Web browsers set to display a particular home page, so whenever we get on the Internet, we are faced with a page filled with the day's news or celebrity gossip or something else that sucks us in and wastes our time. Try setting your default home page to something that is less time-consuming or more practical. If you typically log on just to check email, then set your email login page as your home page. Maybe you simply want to be greeted by a lovely photo instead. You can set your home page to display a picture of the day from a beach or a garden from someplace like www.national geographic.com. Or, if you are looking for a new quick tip on how to get more organized and save even more time, then set your home page to www.jamienovak.com so you can always get the newest ideas. Changing your default home page is simple and saves lots of time; even if you are not computer proficient, you can manage this setup. On most computers, simply log onto the Internet and at the top of your Web browser, click the "Tools" button, then choose "Internet options." Next click on the "General" tab. In the first of three options, type in the website you'd like to make your home page. Don't forget the "http://www" part; it's important! Then click "Apply" and "OK," and you are done.

645. Use the "recently viewed pages" option. This can be done by clicking the small arrow that is located to the right of the bar displaying the website that you are currently viewing. When you click the arrow, it displays a list of the recently viewed websites so you can easily pick one to return to. This is especially helpful if you forgot to bookmark a great site and want to return to it. You can customize the number of days these recently viewed pages are listed for. Follow the above directions for customizing your home page, but on the general tab, instead of typing a new home page in, use the third option and choose the number of days you'd like your history to be displayed (anywhere from 0–99 days). (To keep the list manageable, fifteen days is usually a good bet for the average computer user.)

646. Use instant messaging (IM) sparingly. Sometimes it makes more sense to send an email or even to make an actual phone call to the person you need to reach. There are occasions when an instantaneous conversation works, but think before you IM.

647. Computer games can be addictive; you may find yourself saying, "Just one more game...," without realizing how much time you've lost. Set a timer to limit the length of time you spend gaming. You might also opt to play after you have finished a task you have been putting off doing; that way that game acts as motivation.

648. Block pop-up ads. Most computers offer the option to stop these annoying ads from invading your screen as you attempt to surf the Internet. Opt to block them all immediately.

649. Reduce the time you spend searching online. Use the common search formulas so search engines can return more precise matches. For example, skip common words like "and," "where," and "how." Search engines ignore them anyway, so don't waste time typing them.

650. If a particular common word is important to the search, then you must include it by using the plus sign (+) after a single space. For example, if you want to find information on a specific episode of a television show that has different episode numbers, type the show name, leave a space, and then type a plus sign followed by the number of the episode you are looking for (like this: "my favorite show +301") to find episode 301 of *My Favorite Show*.

651. Remember, most search engines are not case-sensitive. So "Jamie Novak" and "JamIE novaK" will return the same matches.

652. When words have more than one meaning, be sure to specify which term you are looking for. Here's how to do it: type your term, then leave a single space and type the minus sign (-) followed by a word indicating the way you *don't* mean the search terms to be used. For example, if you want to find more information about *My Favorite Show* (the television series) and *not My Favorite Show: The Movie*, then type "my favorite show -movie" to exclude websites that mention "My Favorite Show" and "movie." It's not a perfect method, but most of the time it will do the job.

653. If you are looking for an *exact* match, then put the term or phrase in quotes.

654. Don't forget to try all sorts of variations on the word or term you are trying. If you want information on a specific type of children's clothing and you don't get the response you want, try substituting the word "apparel" or "garment" for clothing.

655. Use the "Favorites" or "Bookmarks" option. When you find a website that is useful and that you might like to return to in the future, simply bookmark it in your Favorites section. Once you are on a website you like (let's say it's www.jamienovak.com), while the page is on your computer screen, click the button on the top of the screen called "Favorites" or "Bookmarks." Then choose the option to "Save" or "Save In." If you click "Save," it will put the website in a single alphabetized list of your favorites, so www.jamienovak.com will show up under the J's. If you choose "Save As," you have the option to change the name of the site, so instead of www.jamienovak.com you might change the name to Time Management Ideas. It as simple as that! It saves tons of time trying to remember websites you like or looking for the piece of paper where you wrote your list. (You can get more complex and give each family member his or her own folder, but start with the basics.)

656. Get to know the icons (small pictures) that are meant to serve as shortcuts. With a single click on the picture of the printer, you can print the web page you are on. And with a single click on the picture of a piece of mail, you can email the web page. Icons are your friends; get to know them well.

657. You can customize your toolbar with the icons you use most often and remove the icons you hardly ever use. (Having trouble seeing the little pictures? Change your computer setting to make the icons larger and much easier to read.)

658. Think before you print. Do you have to print that recipe out and spend time finding a place to store it in case you might want to make it one day, or can you simply bookmark the web page or save the recipe online? Many recipe websites now offer the opportunity to log in at no charge and create an online recipe box where you can store all your favorites. (The same goes for many online retailers as well.) You can even email yourself the page and save it in a folder in your email inbox. These are much easier options than inviting another piece of paper into your life!

36.

Computer/ Blackberry/ PDA

659. Don't put all the icons for all the computer programs on your desktop. For the programs you open often, it makes sense. But for the programs you rarely use, it is easier to locate them from the start button if you're using a PC. This way you save time by being able to easily see and open the commonly used programs.

660. If you have ever had power to your computer knocked out unexpectedly, then you'll know what a time-saver this tip is. Program the computer to auto-save your work every few minutes. That way you won't have to recreate your work if the power goes out. Simply click "Tools" then "Options" then the "Save" tab, and change the number of minutes listed for "auto recover" to somewhere between five to ten minutes.

661. Keep a directions file so you'll spend less time looking up directions to places you need to go. Clearly label the page when you save it, so later you'll know what the directions are for. To save even more time, write out the directions to your home and office one time from all points (north, south, east, and west) then store them on your computer. Whenever you need to give someone directions you can print and mail them a copy or cut and paste them into an email. You might also include a photograph of your home or office along with the directions so it can be easily spotted. Don't forget to include your phone number.

662. Use the original. Instead of drafting a new letter to answer a routine correspondence, simply write the answer on the paper you received, make a copy, and send back the original. Use the same technique for email inquires. Rather than typing a whole new email, cut out the parts of the email you don't need and reuse what was originally sent to you. Try never to delete the original email; simply hit reply, and then leave the original message intact and write your response.

663. When you save a file, don't just save it to your desktop. This will waste your time in the future when you need to locate it, because it will be hard to find. Take a few minutes to set up folders, and then place the documents in the correct folders. If you do not consider yourself computer savvy, don't worry; this is a simple thing to learn, and it will save tons of time—especially if you tend to lose documents and then have to take the time to recreate them. If you are using Microsoft Word, here is how you do this: type your document and when it is time to save it, choose "Save As" from the file menu. A box will pop up; at the top of this box is a window with a down arrow to the right of it. This contains the *folder* where you want this *file* to be saved. Think of the folder as the green hanging folder in a file drawer and the file as the manila folder to be put inside. You can choose "My Documents," for example, as the folder; when you click on that, "My Documents" will stay in the window. Now you could save all your files in My Documents, but you'd have a lot to look through to find what you need. Instead, make another folder inside the My Documents folder. At the top of the "Save As" box, there will be a picture of a yellow file folder *with the starburst in the right corner*; click on it. When you click it, a new manila folder will pop up inside the "Save As" box. Type the name of the folder in the space provided. Make the name something meaningful so you know exactly what is inside. Once you like the name, click anywhere outside the box to save the new folder's name. Then click the file folder you just named—let's say in this case it's "Letters to Insurance"—and that name will appear in the window in the top of the box. Finally, at the bottom of the box you can now type the name of the file, which is what you want to call the document you are saving. In this case it might be "flood claim letter January 2007." Click save and you are done! Next time you want to see that letter, simply click open My Documents, then Letters to Insurance, and then "flood claim letter January 2007."

664. You might find it helpful to give each family member a folder of his or her own, that way each person has a place to store files and will not clutter up your desktop or your folders.

665. When naming the documents, use names that make sense to you so you can find the files again. Remember, you may not look at some of these files again for months, so although a file called "birthday invitation" might make sense today, in a few months you might not know which birthday invitation and have to waste time opening the file only to find out it is not the one you were looking for. "1st birthday invite for Sam 2007" would be more helpful.

666. For your home or work office, it can be extremely helpful to create folders with the names that mirror your paper files. One system makes life easier and saves you time.

667. To avoid wasting time proofreading your document, you can set the computer options to spell check or grammar check for you. (When a word is underlined in red, you can simply roll the mouse over it then right click with the mouse, and a box will pop up with correct spelling choices.)

668. If you have ever accidentally deleted a portion of your document and then spent time recreating it, you'll find that the "Undo" option can be a lifesaver. Whenever you delete something, but then want it back, simply select "Edit" from the Menu at the top of the screen and then click the first choice ("Undo"). This puts back whatever you recently took away. You can click Undo multiple times, and each click will take you back to an earlier version of the document you are working on, undoing whatever changes you most recently made.

669. Instead of retyping text that you want to move in a document, simply use the mouse to highlight the text and then right click it with the mouse. Choose "Cut" and then move the pointer to where you want the text. Right click again and choose "Paste." The text will be inserted for you automatically. (If you want to leave the text in the original spot and simply have the same text appear somewhere else, then instead of choosing "Cut," which deletes it, choose "Copy" and then "Paste." This will duplicate the text, *not* delete it.

670. Stop backspacing over correctly typed words to correct other text. It actually wastes more time to backspace and retype text that was correct than it does to move the cursor and correct just the wrong text. Backspacing is usually just a habit, one that you can break fairly easily.

671. Lost a document? Saved it but not sure where? Or forgot what you named it? No problem. Use the "Search and Find" feature. Click the start button on the lower left side of your screen. Choose "Search" and then type in as much information as you know. Most often you'll want to supply a few keywords you remember from the document. If it was a flyer for the soccer tournament, then type any words that appear on the flyer, "tournament," "soccer," and the date. Then click search. The computer will look through every document and list the ones where those words appear. Then you can look over the list or open each one until you find your lost document.

672. Another time-saving shortcut is the "Find and Replace" feature. This allows you to single out one word or several words and find every occurrence. You can also opt to replace any item with a different word. Let's say you typed a document, and throughout it you spelled your Aunt Shelley's name incorrectly: S-h-e-l-l-y instead of S-h-e-l-l-e-y. When you're finally finished typing the entire document, you realize she spells it "Shelley." Instead of spending time replacing each one individually, you can choose the "Find" function and instruct the computer to replace each "Shelly" with "Shelley."

673. Most software programs come pre-programmed with templates that you can use. Let's say you want a fax cover sheet. You can opt to use one of the templates provided for you to customize. Before you reinvent the wheel, check to see if what you need already exists.

674. Don't forget to consider documents you've already typed as templates as well. This means if you need to type a letter, instead of making a whole new one, you can open an old letter and modify it. (When you open an old document and modify it you will have two choices for saving it. You can choose "Save," which will overwrite the original document with the newer version. Or you can choose "Save As," which leaves the original intact and simply creates a new file with a new file name for the newest document. Not sure which one you need? Then play it safe, and choose Save As; this is the safest bet since it leaves the original intact and creates a new file for the new document.)

675.

The auto-correct feature allows you to tell the computer to type a specific word or phrase when you type a shorter version of that word or phrase. For example, if your name is Samantha K. Worthington, that can be a lot to type each time you want your full name to appear. Instead of wasting time with all those keystrokes, simply program the computer to know that when you type "SK" it should automatically change it to "Samantha K. Worthington." To do this, go to "Tools" and select "Auto Correct." Then, in the box that pops up, type your abbreviation and type what you would like it to be replaced with. In this example the abbreviation would be "SK" and the text for it to be replaced with is "Samantha K. Worthington." You can remove the abbreviation from the list anytime you choose to. (When choosing your abbreviation, make it uncommon. Telling the computer to replace the letters "TO" with "Tom Kinney," for example, is a bad idea since the computer can't distinguish between the word "to" and your abbreviation. You can use whatever combination of letters you want for your abbreviation, so using something like "QW" for "Tom Kinney" would be a safe bet.)

676. If you need to sort a list by certain criteria, say alphabetically, you can do this automatically by choosing the Sort button under the "Table" menu or by clicking the Sort icon (the letters A and Z with an arrow).

677. Here are a few shortcuts to save you time when you want to underline a word, bold lines of text, or italicize: use the icons on the toolbar. The dark letter B is for bolding type, the italics I is for italicizing, and the underlined U is for underlining.

678. To change the size of the font (a fancy word for type or the way the letters look), use the window at the top of the page with the number in it and a down arrow to the side of it. When you click the arrow, it offers a list of font sizes to choose from. The bigger the number, the bigger the type. Twelve-point font is an average size suitable for most documents. If you'd like to adjust the style of the type, use the window with the name of the font style in it that also has a down arrow next to it. When you click the arrow you are given a list of font styles to choose from. Lastly, to change the color of the font, use the icon that is a letter "A" with a bar of color under it; this also has a down arrow next to it. When you click the arrow, a box will pop up with all the colors of the rainbow to choose from. Once you click the color you want, the bar under the letter A in the icon changes to the color you selected. To make a change to any text, simply highlight it, and then click the icon corresponding to the action you want to perform.

679. If you have a typed list that you want to number or add bullet points to, you can simply highlight the text and click the appropriate icon. The icon with the numbers 1, 2, and 3 on it is for numbered lists. The icon with a set of three bullet points with lines after them is for adding bullets to a list.

680. A quick way to justify your text—either flush left, flush right, centered, or fully justified—is to highlight the text and use the icons related to each justification. The flush left icon shows a bunch of lines all lined up to the left with a ragged right edge. The flush right icon displays just the opposite. For centered text, choose the icon with the lines centered, giving ragged right and left edges. Lastly, the fully justified icon shows the lines that are fully flush left and right.

681. Want a quick way to find the last few files you were working on? Click "File" on the menu bar, and at the bottom of the box that comes up, there will be a list of the last four files that were open on your computer. You can click the name of the one you want to open.

682. Not sure how to find some of these features? Use the help button. Click help and then type in your question. Related matches will come up, and you can pick the answer you are looking for.

683. Once you learn how to take advantage of one or more of these features, make yourself a cheat sheet. Write the steps out and post them near the computer so you can refer to them without having to look up the instructions each time you want to perform the function.

684. The orb is a product you can buy and plug into your computer that will change colors based on the criteria you set up. For example, you might program it to change to red when the news reports traffic on your regular route; that way you can stay informed without even logging onto the Internet. You can find the orb at www.ambientdevices.com.

HAVE MORE TIME TODAY!

1. Treat your email like your paper mail, and only check the inbox one or two times a day.
2. Learn how to save items on your computer so you can stop printing out so much paper.
3. Set up a folder for you and each family member in which each person can store his or her own documents.

TRY THIS:

Stop email overload by setting aside time during the day to process emails instead of simply reading through them.

REPEAT AFTER ME:

"I do what I can during the time I've set aside for the task. When the buzzer goes off, done or not done, I move on to the next task."

Part Thirteen:

When Unplugging Is Not an Option

According to Nielsen Media Research, the average American watches more than four hours of TV each day (or twenty-eight hours per week). That's two months of nonstop TV-watching per year. In sixty-five years, the average American will have spent the equivalent of nine straight years glued to the tube! To date, no one has performed a conclusive study to confirm how many hours are wasted by those of us who can't seem to get our digital camera pictures downloaded to our computers!

37.
Phones

685. Stop giving your cell phone number to just anyone. You don't need to be accessible to *everyone* all the time. Constant calls break your concentration, force you to multitask, and never allow you to have a break from being available. You can block your number so the people you call are unable to see your cell number; that way, people you don't want to have your number can't see it. To block your home phone number from appearing on people's caller IDs when you call them, dial *70 (in most cases) before dialing their numbers; this is a service offered free by most carriers.

686. Place your cordless phone back in its charging base when finished with it, and make a habit of plugging your cell phone into the charger when you come in the door. You won't waste any more time looking for them since you'll always know where they are; plus, they'll always be charged and ready when you need them.

687. Program your cell phone with commonly dialed phone numbers. Having the numbers preprogrammed means less time trying to locate a person's phone number. Emergency personnel recommend that you program in a phone number under the name "ICE" (in case of emergency) to be called in the event of an emergency. Professionals are being trained to look in the address books of cell phones for an ICE number. You can program more than one number by using ICE, ICE2, ICE3, and so on.

688. When you program numbers into your cell phone, most arrange themselves alphabetically. This means if you call Sally often, you need to scroll through the list to get to the S's. Save time by adding an "A" or "1" in front of Sally's name; for example, "A Sally." This puts her name among the first in the list. (You can use the same trick for names that are all of a same category. For example, you may want to program in your favorite restaurants. Instead of doing it by name only and having them scattered throughout the entire list, simply add an "R" (your code for restaurants) in front of each of the names: "R Alfredo's," "R Bistro," "R Clam Shack," etc.

689. If you find yourself hunting in the bottom of your handbag for your cell phone, try placing it in a cell phone holder with a strap. Wrap the strap around the handle of your handbag, with the cell phone inside your bag—that way you'll always have it handy.

690. Learn your phone's features. Phones offer many time-saving options that you can only take advantage of if you know how to use them. Take a moment to learn the features. (Don't have time to read the manual? Carry it with you, and read a page at a time or dial the toll-free customer service line and ask them to walk you through some of the best options. That is what they are there for, and they know the phones better than anyone.)

691. Customize your ringtones so you know right away if it's your sister or your boss calling. That way you'll know if you need to stop what you are doing to pick up the phone or call back later.

692. Use the alarm option on your cell phone to remind yourself of important dates like birthdays or to do things like leave for an appointment or make a phone call.

TEN TRICKS TO BYPASS AUTO-MATED ANSWERING SERVICES

1. *, #, or 0 have a good chance of working, although sometimes this will simply disconnect you.
2. Speak. Many answering services use voice recognition so you can ask for a representative or an agent or customer service.
3. Don't yell; this distorts your voice so the other person can't understand you.
4. Do not mumble. The voice recognition software won't be able to understand you and will connect you with an agent.
5. Stay on hold without pressing any buttons; the phone service will assume you have a rotary phone and connect you to a customer service representative or the operator.
6. Select the Spanish-speaking agent option, and you'll get a bilingual agent much faster than you would an English-only agent.
7. Use the non-800 phone number; the hold time

is usually less.

8. Choose the wrong option and ask the agent to stay on the line while he or she connects you directly; you'll jump ahead in the queue.

9. Call at nonpeak times.

10. Visit www.gethuman.com, and refer to the database for specific instructions for various companies.

693. Put a stop to those pesky telemarketers who always call at the wrong time. Simply register all of your phone numbers (home, cell, and others) for free at www.donot call.gov. It only takes a moment. Provide up to three phone numbers at a time and your email address. You will receive an email which you *must* open. Once you click the link in the email, your phone number will be protected for five years. This service is provided *free of charge* by the Federal Trade Commission. (Prefer to call instead of going online? Dial 1-888-382-1222.) Not sure if you already registered your number? Call or go online and choose the "verify a registration" option.)

694. Save time running up and down the stairs in your home to grab the phone when it rings. Have at least one phone on every floor.

695. Place a carbon copy, spiral-bound phone message pad near each of the phones in your house. Then make it a household rule that messages need to be written down there. Place the original in a designated location so the person will see it. Leave the carbon copy in the spiral book. That way if the original is lost or you need to refer back to the message, you will have it on hand.

696. Take advantage of the speakerphone and headset features on your phone, if available. Either of these allows you to work hands free while talking on the phone or on hold; you can open the mail, put away groceries, or fold laundry.

697. Designate a telephone hour during which you return and make phone calls. This allows you to do this task at a prime time for you; it might be making dinner while using a headset or walking your dog while using your cell phone.

698. Use your answering machine to screen calls. This allows you to return the calls at a more convenient time for you. Just because the phone rings doesn't mean you have to answer it.

699. Program your home phones and fax (if you have one) with speed dial numbers. The short amount of time it takes to program the machine is made up for since each time you need to make a call, you save keystrokes. (Once you've read the manual and know how to do it, jot down the steps or make a photocopy of the manual page and hang it nearby so you won't have to reread the manual if you want to make changes in the future.)

700. Don't be afraid to simply say, "I'd love to chat, but I can't right now. Can I call you back?" You don't have to make excuses.

701. When calling a company, after reaching a live person, the first thing you should do is ask for his or her name and the direct number to reach him or her in case you are disconnected for any reason.

702. Minimize time spent playing telephone tag. Ask the person when the best time to return the call is, so you'll have the best chance of reaching them.

703. Go with caller ID. When you can see who is calling, it is much easier to screen the callers and only pick up the calls you want to.

704. If you are too rushed for a long chat with an old friend, but still want to make contact, or if you don't have time to get caught on the phone with a chatty friend, simply send her a text message. It will allow you to keep in touch without wasting time. (Use text messaging wisely; sometimes it takes more time to exchange multiple messages than it would to simply call the person.)

38.
Television

705. Want to gain fifty-two hours each year? Simply turn off the television for one more hour a week than you normally would. Presto! Fifty-two hours to spare!

706. Turn the television off right after your show ends; don't get sucked into the next program.

707. Opt for turning on the radio instead of the television. Since radio just requires that you listen instead of listen *and* watch, you are better able to multitask while the radio is on.

708. If you have children who love to watch television, try implementing a household rule of TV-time tickets. Much as they would with tickets used to gain entrance to an amusement park ride, children can turn in their TV tickets in exchange for television time. For example, if the new family rule is seven hours a week, then print fourteen tickets for a half hour each and give them to the child at the start of the week. They can then turn in one ticket for each half hour of television they want to watch. When the tickets are gone, there is no more television until the next week. (This may seem radical, but try it for a week or two; children get the hang of it quickly and find more creative ways to spend their time. Exemptions to the rule might be movies or shows watched as a family.)

709. By recording your favorite programs and fast-forwarding through the commercials, you can save a significant amount of time.

710. Stop hunting for your remotes. Choose one spot for the remotes to live, and always return them when finished. A decorative basket on an end table or a drawer in the coffee table may work well.

39.

Photos and Cameras

711. Learn how to use your camera. Whether you prefer to read the manual, have the salesperson walk you through the options, take a community school class, or call the company directly and ask the customer service representative, pick a way to learn how to use it. This will save you lots of time.

712. Before storing away cords and wires, take an extra moment to label them. Jot down what each is used for and today's date, so in the future you can refer to the list to remind yourself how long ago it was you bought the item and what the chances are you still own it. (Masking tape wrapped directly around the cord can make a handy label.)

713. Label the cords before you plug them into a socket. The next time you unplug a cord you'll know which one it is instead of having to pull on a cord to see what it is attached to.

714. A large ziplock bag is a perfect storage place for the accessories and the instruction manual. Place them in the bag, label the bag, and tuck it away. You might also place your purchase receipt in the bag. (You might also want to fold down the box it came in and keep that in there as well. That way if you need to return or exchange it, you'll have everything you need in one place.)

715. Save time when filling out the warranty card. Instead of trying to squeeze your name onto the little lines they provide on the form, simply stick a return address label on that section and mail it in.

716. Avoid wasting valuable time sorting through boxes of photos trying to locate the one you are looking for; make it easier to put away new photos by organizing them.

717. If you plan to scrapbook, save time by keeping all your supplies in one place, ready to be used. That way when you have the time to work on the project, you don't waste it gathering the items you need to get the job done.

718. Choosing to organize and/or scrapbook your photos in manageable chunks of time will keep you from feeling overwhelmed by your photos. Do not plan to work on all your photos at one time; if you think "all or nothing," you'll never start because it will feel so unmanageable.

719. As you look through developed photographs, be *very* selective as to what you hold onto. Only keep the photos that are flattering and in focus. By eliminating the duplicates or bad shots you will automatically have fewer photos to deal with. (When taking photos, avoid taking five consecutive shots of the same thing, unless it is a potentially priceless shot like those taken at a wedding.)

720. Choose one way to sort your photographs, and stick with it. By having a single way to keep the photos in order, you won't have to figure out how to organize each new batch, and you will save time when you are trying to locate one in the pile. Organizing chronologically is the most popular choice and saves the most time when getting them in order. (As you sort the photos, take a moment and pop a sticky note onto the backs of the photos for which you remember the names of the people or the story around the photo. Jotting down the information when you remember it means you won't have to struggle trying to recall it later on.)

IT WORKED FOR HER

"I use software to sort and organize digital photos similarly to the physical box. There are many features and benefits to the software."

Sandra Donofrio, NJ

721. Label each and every photo container and envelope. Knowing what is in each and every container and envelope will make finding photos easy. Plus, if you choose to scrapbook some or all of them, you'll be able to find the ones you need.

722. When using your digital camera, make it a habit to download the photos immediately when you get home. If you print your photos at home, you should do that right away as well. Putting off the task until later will turn a relatively quick job into a very long job that you will continue to put off since it will feel unmanageable. (When taking digital photos, delete the poor ones right after you review them. No sense holding onto them if you don't love them.)

723. Consider trying one of the mail away services for getting your film developed. Even if you use a digital camera, you can still use a service like this. You simply go to the company's website to upload the pictures you want to be printed, and they print them and mail them to you. Additionally, there are now services where you can upload the pictures and have them developed at a brand name pharmacy anywhere in the United States. This means you can have family members and friends pick them up and you won't have to develop and mail them. Note: Shutterfly, Mystic Color Labs, Snapfish, and Kodak are four mail-order processing companies you might consider checking out—most offer first-time user discounts and specials.

724. Save time filling out the envelopes to have your film developed by carrying a few return address labels with you and sticking those on instead of handwriting the information on the envelope. Additionally, if you tend to get your film developed at the same location, take a few envelopes home with you and fill them out so the next time you have a roll of film ready for developing, you can simply pop it in an envelope that is ready to go.

725. Designate a single location to keep film that needs to be developed. Instead of dropping the rolls into a drawer and letting them pile up, keep on top of the photos by having one place to keep the rolls and taking them with you when you run other errands.

726. If photo organizing is a true priority for you right now, then pull out your calendar and schedule time each and every month to work on the photos. Unless you set aside time to get the job done, it will just be another task you set aside to do later; and later may never come. If it is not a priority, then release the guilt you may feel about not getting your photos in order. You're busy making memories, not scrapbooking them, and that is okay.

727. When you download your digital photos, rename them with names that you can easily recognize. The computer usually names them with a series of number and/or letters, but these will not hold any meaning for you. So to avoid having to look through hundreds of photos to find the one you want, give them a name that is meaningful. Rename photo "XYZ123" to "Erik and Kiara flying kite July 2006," which is specific enough to help you know if this is the photo you are looking for. (Use photo-organizing software to keep digital photos in folders by date or category.)

728. Keep a box of spare photos on hand that your children can use for school projects. When they need photos of themselves for an autobiography project, you will not have to spend time locating pictures and making duplicates that they can cut.

729. Carry a small project tote bag with a photo album and an envelope of photos with you. Whenever you have a few spare moments, like while waiting for a meeting to begin, sitting in the waiting room in your physician's office, or waiting to pick your child up from sports practice, you can pop a few more photos into the album.

730.

Save time in the long run by protecting and preserving your treasured photographs from disaster, temperature changes, and computer crashes. This means storing photos in boxes that are sunlight-proof and using acid-free albums. Never use "magnetic" albums; you'll end up wasting lots of valuable time unsticking the photos from the pages with a special adhesive dissolving solution.

HAVE MORE TIME TODAY!

1. Try screening your phone calls.
2. Turn off the television as soon as your show is over so you are not sucked into watching the next thing that comes on.
3. Learn the features of your camera.

TRY THIS:

Set up a new system for all the new photographs you will take. Then, in small blocks of time, work on getting any backlog of photos in order.

REPEAT AFTER ME:

"I get more pleasure from making new memories than worrying about organizing old ones."

Part Fourteen:

Are You Costing Yourself
a Raise and a Promotion?

Whether you work in an office and then come home to act as the "CEO of your home" or you are a full-time, home-based CEO with or without another home-based business, you know time is money. A wonderful way to illustrate this point is to figure out what *your* time is worth; once you know, you will be less likely to waste another minute. Here's a quick equation: take your yearly salary and divide it by the average number of hours you work (or want to work) in a year; if you work forty hour weeks, then it is about 1,920 hours with holidays and two weeks of vacation. To calculate the value of each minute, take the hourly wage you calculated and divide it by sixty. For example, if your goal is to make $80,000 per year while working twenty-five hours per week (for fifty-two weeks), divide $80,000 by 1,300, which amounts to an hourly rate of $61.50 an hour and a per-minute rate of $1.02. Knowing that an extra couple minutes reading junk mail or talking on the phone with a telemarketer will cost you over two dollars can help you manage your time more wisely.

40.

The Floor Is Not an Option

731. Whenever you are given a business card, take a moment to jot the date on the card. Later on you'll know how current the information is. Try filing the cards in a Rolodex by category since you might not always remember a person's name or the name of the business; the category is much easier. Save time by sliding the card into a prepunched plastic Rolodex sleeve or stapling it to a Rolodex card instead of recopying the information.

732. Store personal mementos like framed photographs off your desk. It always takes more time to find things when there is a lot to look around, so keep only essential items at hand.

733. A great way to keep things off your desk but still visible is to hang a decorative clothesline nearby. This will allow you to hang up notes, personal photographs, commonly referenced information, and other items you want handy but that tend to get lost when stacked in a pile on your desk.

734. Write in red ink on the tab of your file folders the date after which you can toss the file. This will act as your discard date, so you can avoid spending time sorting through the file later on to determine whether or not you need to keep it.

735. Limit the quantity of supplies you jam in your desk drawers. Instead, keep the excess stock in another location and refill from there. When you crowd drawers with excess supplies, you end up wasting time digging around for what you need.

736. Leave yourself notes with helpful information on how and where to reorder supplies. Let's say you order model number 123 fax toner cartridges from XYZ Company. Since you don't order them all that often, you might find yourself spending time searching for the information the next time you need to place an order. Instead, leave a note taped to the last cartridge so that when you open that box, you'll have all the information for ordering right there at your fingertips.

737. Make yourself cheat sheets for tasks. For example, if you don't send faxes very often, you might forget which way the paper should face whenever you attempt to send a fax, which means you'll have to waste time finding the manual or experimenting. Instead, tape a little set of instructions to the fax machine, or photocopy the page from the instruction manual and post it nearby.

41.
Meetings

738. Whenever possible, send a representative to a meeting in your place and have him or her report back to you. If that is not an option, ask if the meeting can be recorded so that you can listen to it as you work or commute.

739. Opt for conference calls instead of in-person meetings whenever possible. With all the new technology, including Web and video conferencing equipment, you don't need to be in the same room to meet with a group of people.

740. Choose to have the meeting at one of the most productive times of day; it will be shorter, and everyone will retain more of the information. Meetings first thing in the morning are generally a better idea than at three in the afternoon when people's focus is lessened. (Try having everyone stand and stretch every thirty minutes; attention spans are only about that long.)

741. If the meeting will be brief, conduct it standing up. It will be less formal and go faster. To save even more time, only invite the necessary people; the fewer people attending, the faster the meeting goes.

742. Prior to the meeting, pass out written agendas with a time frame for each topic to be discussed. Place the start time and end time on the agenda. Make a note in bold if someone is responsible for bringing something to the meeting. (Designate someone as the timekeeper; this person will also be responsible for keeping the meeting on track. Rotate this duty from meeting to meeting.)

743. Make one person responsible for taking notes and distributing them within forty-eight hours of the meeting. Make sure action items are noted in bold.

744. At the start of the meeting, request that everyone turn off their cell phones and turn pagers to vibrate. The fewer interruptions, the faster things can move along.

745. Add a question-and-answer period at the end of the meeting. Let people know it is coming so they will save all their questions until then. Often, their questions will all have been answered sometime during the meeting before the Q&A period begins.

746. If someone has a very specific question, ask to speak with them about it one-on-one after the meeting. That way the meeting stays on track, and others are not held captive to a conversation that does not involve them.

747. At the end of the meeting, take time for a quick recap of what was discussed and who is responsible for doing what. Having everyone in one room at the same time to catch missed or doubled assignments or incorrect timelines will save countless hours in the long run.

42.

Automate Processes

748. Maximize your voice mail message by recording a message that is more useful to callers. For instance, you can mention which hour of the day you typically return calls so they know when to expect your call. You can ask callers to leave a message and tell you the best time to call them back, lessening the chances of phone tag. You can also mention whom to call for immediate assistance and whom to call for other issues; for example, if people often call you when they really should be calling your coworker, provide that person's contact information. Lastly, make sure you include information you are commonly asked for, like your fax number or website address.

749. When you need to stop working on a project, post a sticky note on the file or paperwork, so that when you resume work on it, you will know exactly what the next step is and you won't have to spend any time backtracking.

750. When passing a project on to a coworker or assistant, post a sticky note on it first. Jot down a message with the action you need the person to take; this cuts down on miscommunication and minimizes the time he or she needs to spend figuring out what the next step is.

751. Create checklists of the tasks you perform. Keeping these checklists in a binder will act as your own personal reference guide. Whenever you need to refresh your memory about how to do a task, you'll have your own guidelines. (When the checklists are put together, they create an outline for your procedure manual, and they also serve as a job description—especially around raise time to show management all your duties.)

752. Store all those contact phone lists, schedules, and other commonly referenced papers in a three ring binder near your desk. Save more time by sliding the pages into top-loading, clear plastic sheet protectors instead of punching holes in each paper.

753. If you find yourself spending time letting people know that you did indeed receive their emails and are following up appropriately on your end, you can opt to have the email system send an automatic reply to the sender. You can customize this automatic reply to say something like, "Your email has been received, and I am in the process of working on it. You can expect a response within the next day, unless you have indicated that you need a response sooner than that. Thank you."

754. Instead of spending time typing your name, extension, and other routine information at the end of every email, you can have it automatically added to each email before it is sent by setting up a signature line. A great time-saving use for this option is also to include answers to frequently asked questions, so the recipients will not have to get in touch with you directly for the answers. (You can opt to have more than one signature line, and then just select the one you want to use for each particular email you send; this is still faster than retyping all the information.)

755. Learn to use the features on your printer. For example, instead of spending time printing labels and then sticking them onto envelopes, learn how to insert the envelopes for direct printing. A little time spent up front saves tons of time and effort in the long run. If your company has an IT department, you can always ask them for a brief tutorial.

756. To ensure that you will leave work on time, ask a coworker whom you've noticed always leaves at a reasonable hour to stop by your desk on his or her way out, and then you two can walk out together.

HAVE MORE TIME TODAY!

1. Move extra chairs away from your desk to keep you from dumping stuff on them or having people stop by to chat.
2. Try having quick meetings standing up—once everyone sits down it is more comfortable, making it easier to linger a little too long. Try walking and talking with someone as you both go for a cup of coffee.
3. Post directions for machines nearby, so you don't have to reread the manual each time.

TRY THIS:

Use your commute, no matter how long or short, productively. There are many things besides work that can be considered productive. You can choose to listen to relaxing music or a book on tape. Or you can opt for quiet time; simply turn off the radio and clear your mind.

REPEAT AFTER ME:

"Fifteen minutes before I want to leave work I wrap up so I can leave on time."

Part Fifteen:

I Just Saw It a Minute Ago

The average person wastes ninety minutes a day looking for lost or misplaced items! That's a lot of wasted time! What if you could get back at least a few of those lost minutes?

43.

Clutter Control Step One: Like with Like

757. Work in eighteen-minute blocks of time when organizing a space. Instead of waiting for a huge block of free time, which rarely comes along, try focusing on a task for a short period of time. Set a timer and get down to business. When the buzzer goes off you can set it for another eighteen, or walk away from the project knowing you made progress and you have a plan for finishing the job.

758. A sure way to make things worse is to pull everything out of the space without enough time to put it all back. Instead, work on a small section at a time, and only pull out a portion of stuff from the area; if you pull it all out, you won't be able to put it back and the space will be worse than when you started. The one exception is when you are working on a large project like clearing the garage, and you have lots of hours and lots of help. That's an all-day job, and you can afford to take everything out at once to get it done right.

759. If you do have a longer block of time, like a few hours, then go for that long. The goal is small, consistent blocks of time, but if you ever have more time to give to the project, go ahead. Just be sure, no matter how long you have, that you reserve enough time at the end to tidy up; you do not want to leave the items spread all over the place—that's just more mess you'll have to spend time cleaning up or working around.

760. Have your supplies on hand *before* you get started so you will not have to leave the area to get something; if you leave you can get sidetracked and have a hard time getting back to the project. Items like garbage bags, a pen and paper, a timer, water, the phone (if you will be tempted to go check who is calling), and empty boxes or laundry baskets to sort into should be kept nearby.

761. What should you be doing during those eighteen minutes? Grouping like items together. Your job at this point is to find out exactly what you have, not to decide what to keep and what to toss—that comes later. I want you to go in phases. Since getting started is usually the most difficult part of the process, I want you to start with the easiest task, putting like items together. If you have a hard time deciding what to group together, think of a store and what would be in each aisle. In a shoe store, all the dressy shoes might be in one aisle and all the sneakers in another, so make two piles—one for each type of shoe. You can't really do this wrong, so get started and give it a try.

762. While going through the area, you are bound to come across an unidentifiable item or two; you simply have no idea what it is or even to whom it belongs. Instead of trying to figure it out, simply make an "I don't know what this is" pile. This will help you to stay on track with the job at hand.

763. You may also come across items that you borrowed or that someone left at your house. Make a pile of "things to be given back to their owners." Later, you can sort through the pile and match each item with its owner.

764. While doing this step, some people report coming across things that need to be returned, things like an overdue library book, a blouse that doesn't fit, and so on. You guessed it—make another pile of "things to be returned."

765. "Things to be done" will be another pile you will probably end up having to make. This will be for all the things you come across that need your attention. This pile is most popular when you are sorting through paperwork, since you are bound to find undone projects in the pile of papers.

766. Whenever you come across an item that needs fixing, pop it in the "fix me" pile. A dress that needs mending, a ripped book cover that needs tape, a game that needs its batteries replaced, and other items that need some sort of repair can go in this pile.

767. Lastly, make another pile of things that belong in another room. Remember, I suggested that you don't leave the area where you are working. Just make a pile while you work, and distribute the items once your eighteen minutes are up.

768. You might wonder why I am suggesting you make all these small piles. Well, it is in keeping with the theme of "like with like." All of these smaller piles have something in common. If you were to lump them all together, you'd only have to sort them out again at a later date.

769. This is not the time to make a big decision about what to keep and what to toss. That is too challenging at this stage since you don't yet know what you own. Instead, find out what you have by sorting through it; then you can figure out what to keep and what to give to a new home.

770. You may come across things that you know for sure can be tossed in the trash; keep a garbage bag handy for these items, and be sure to dump it at the end of your time. Try not to keep garbage bags around in the space. They only add more clutter, and they tempt you to rummage back through them. Plus, you can end up accumulating so many, that taking them out to the garbage seems like an overwhelming task.

771. You may come across gently used things that you know can be given away. Put those aside in their own bag clearly marked for charity; if you have two bags going, one for garbage and one for charity, you won't want to mix those up.

772. Once you have the piles, it will be easy to see what all you have and to work from a place of abundance. You'll see how many duplicates you have of various items, and you can keep the best and toss the rest.

773. At the end of the time, eighteen minutes or more, be sure to tidy up and leave things at least as good as you found them.

774. It can be very helpful to take a picture of the space before you start and then photos of your progress as you work, and then, when you're done, a final "after" shot. This will be your motivation to keep it clear, and when the going gets tough, you can refer to the pictures and see the difference all your hard work is making.

775. It can be very helpful to leave the last thing you were going to do undone so that when you come back to the task, you can easily see what the next step is, and it is easier to get back on a roll. For example, if you are clearing boxes off a shelf, stop before you take down the last box. When you come back, you'll know exactly where to begin, and you'll be more motivated to get back to work. If it will be some time before you can get back to the task, then it can be helpful to leave yourself a little note to remind you where to pick up.

776. Label as you go. This is *very* important. Since things in a pile look the same, you might confuse the giveaway bag with the trash bag, and you'll waste time digging through it all trying to figure out what is what.

44.
Clutter Control Step Two: Put Away Just What You Use and Love

777. Keep the best, and toss the rest. You'll need to pare down to just what you use and love. This means asking yourself some tough questions and being very honest about what you actually use. As you organize, ponder these questions: "When is the last time I used this?" "Do I own something similar?" "Is this really my style?" "Would someone else get more joy from owning it or use it more than I do?" "Does it still fit?" "Is it in good repair, with all its pieces, and do I know how to use it?"

778. Make it easy to find what you already own, so you can stop wasting time and money buying duplicates. Give everything a home and put it back when you are done, so you can find it the next time you need it.

779. Eliminate clutter hot spots by storing items where you use them. Have you ever noticed that when you leave something out, other things tend to congregate around it almost immediately so you have even more to put away later? Often, we'll put something down with every intention of putting it away later, but we never get around to it. By creating storage where things naturally fall, we can eliminate the extra step of putting them away later, since it will be so convenient to just put them away when we are done with them. For example, when you are done hanging a picture frame on the wall, put the screwdriver away in a conveniently located tool chest in the kitchen instead of setting it down until you have the time to walk it back out to the tool area in the garage.

780. Avoid having to make multiple phone calls to local charities to pick up your donations by scheduling a standing appointment with them. The bonus to this will be that since you know they are coming, you will be sure to have a bag ready.

781. Store items where you use them to eliminate wasted trips from room to room to find what you need. For example, if you tend to brush your teeth right before you walk out the door, then keeping a second toothbrush and toothpaste in a downstairs bathroom would make sense, eliminating the need to run upstairs to brush your teeth. Not only will you save time looking for what you need, but you'll also avoid forgetting why you went into the other room in the first place and getting so distracted that the task takes twice as long as it should.

782. Label everything. Labeling bins, baskets, shelves, drawers, and containers saves lots of time in two ways. First, you can find what you need at a glance, and second, you'll be less tempted to place an item where it doesn't belong, since, believe it or not, it is our natural tendency to put things where they belong. The label will deter us from allowing certain places to become catchalls.

783. Commit one key principal to memory: "like with like." Always group similar items together. Here are a few examples: store all the bills in the same place and away from other mail; keep all your jeans in one area of your closet so you can always find them; use one shelf to store all the library books, and keep them separate from the books you own.

784. Measure before buying organizing supplies. You can waste a whole lot of time shopping for and buying containers and products that do not fit as you planned. Then you either have to spend more time returning them or risk losing the money.

785. Set par levels for how much stuff of a certain kind you will keep and how long you will hold onto things. Once you have determined these guidelines for your own home, then you can simply apply them and avoid lengthy debates about what to keep and what to toss. For example, if you decide to subscribe to only three monthly magazines at a time, then you'll never have to spend time deciding if you should subscribe to a fourth. Or, if you know you only have space to store twelve spare rolls of paper towels, then even if there is a super sale, you will not be tempted to purchase more than you can store.

786. Make yourself a treasure box. This will be the one box or container where you can feel free to store all the memories of years gone by: vacation souvenirs, favorite well-worn T-shirts, playbills. Having a home for all your beloved memories will alleviate the need to deliberate for extended periods of time over whether or not to hold onto an item for sentimental reasons. (Giving each person in the house his or her own treasure box is a good idea.)

787. If you find yourself spending lots of time debating about holding onto items that you *might* use one day, then give yourself a "maybe box." Place items in this box that you are fairly certain you will not miss, but that you have a nagging feeling might be useful one day. Tape the box shut; write the contents on the outside of the box along with an expiration date of six to twelve months in the future. Then store the box away. If you need the items, you'll have them, and if by the date on the box you have not gone to the box for anything, give the entire box away *without* looking inside.

788. Post the phone numbers and hours for local charities in a handy location. You can even make a note of what they do and do not accept. That way, when you have a bag of items to pass onto someone who will use and love them, you will not have to hunt around for the information. Also, familiarize yourself with other options such as www.freecycle.org. (For a current list of donation locations visit www.jamienovak.com.)

789. If you prefer to sell an item, you might want to look at a more time-efficient option than setting up a yard sale. Unless yard sales are a fun event for you, you might consider an online sales site such as www.ebay.com. If you are not thrilled with the idea of all the work it takes to sell something online, then consider dropping it off at one of the storefront businesses that will do the work for you and write you a check (minus their commission) when your item sells. Another useful sales site (without any fees for selling) is www.craigslist.org.

790. Clutter Swap parties are a fantastic way to socialize while parting with some of the items you do not use or love, and you may even pick up something you will use and love. Make a list of friends and family to invite and send them an e-vite (www.evite.com) so you don't have to write out invitations. Instruct them to bring a specific number of items with them, and when they arrive, have everyone display their items in the "store," which you can make by using a different space for each area of the store. After drinks and hors d'oeuvres, everyone can shop and refill the bags they brought. At the end of the night, pack up the items not taken and donate them to a local charity.

45.
Clutter Control Step Three: Maintain the New System

791. Once you have made the effort to organize a space, you want it to stay organized, right? You don't want to waste your time and effort reorganizing, so make the effort to *keep it that way.*

792. Utilizing the two-minute rule is a great way to keep things from getting out of control. The two-minute rule says that if you can do a task in two minutes or less, complete it right then. Imagine how many ways you can work this into your day, which means less stuff will be waiting for your attention. You can RSVP to an event, hang up your jacket when you walk in the door, put the glass directly in the dishwasher instead of leaving it in the sink, sort through the mail and toss the junk, shred a handful of sensitive papers, and so much more.

793. Leave room to grow. You will save yourself lots of time by always leaving room to add more items. When you do get more stuff, which usually happens, you'll have a place to put it without reorganizing. Let's say you straightened up your bookshelf, parting with a handful of books and putting all the others away. If the last book just squeezed in, when you get one more book, you'll either have nowhere to put it (so it becomes clutter) or you'll have to spend time reworking the bookshelf.

794. Set up new household rules that everyone agrees with; something as simple as "if you spill it, you wipe it up" can be a huge time-saver.

795. Despite your best efforts, some things will just end up being left out. Dealing with a small amount of this daily will save you from having to spend entire days dealing with the piles. Choose a time to spot organize every day; make it a part of your daily routine.

796. Remember: The less you buy, the less you have to care for, store, and clean around.

797. Organizing is different than cleaning. We make time to clean on a regular basis, but rarely do we make organizing part of the routine. Don't wait until the area is officially declared a disaster zone before you decide to organize. Integrate some clutter-clearing time into your monthly calendar.

798. Tune up your system once a year. You change. Your life changes. How you spend time or how much time you need for different things changes. So check in with yourself yearly and adjust. The systems you devise to meet your needs today may need to be adjusted from time to time.

799. Don't bring home free stuff! Would you want it as badly if you had to pay for it? Probably not.

Part Sixteen:

Getting and Keeping It Together

When you have clutter, everything takes longer. It takes longer to find things, to clean around things, to store things, to worry about things, and so on. Whether you have a small pile of paper on your kitchen countertop or you have lots of stuff piled everywhere, clutter will distract you and cause you to feel overwhelmed. But there is something you can do about it! Here are some simple clutter-clearing techniques that will help you find what you need when you need it!

46.

Everyday Organizing Solutions

800. Stop running around delivering items from the room where they were left to the rooms in the house where they belong. Instead, choose one basket as the mover. As you go from room to room, carry the mover basket with you; put away items from the basket that belong in the room you are in, and place items for other rooms in the mover basket to be put away when you get to the appropriate room.

801. Hang a small basket at both the top and bottom of your staircase. Place items in the basket that need to go up or down, and take them when you go instead of wasting time making a separate trip. (The only way for this will be successful is if you make it a rule to carry it up and down when you go, and you do not use it as catchall where you put things until you have time to get to them later. "Later" will never come.)

802. Those *without* a mudroom would consider you lucky if you have one. But people with mudrooms often complain that it is the hardest room to keep organized. Since a mudroom is used multiple times every day, it is imperative that systems are in place to capture all the stuff. A great model to use for organizing the mudroom is a child's kindergarten classroom. Think of the cubbies with hooks for jackets and shelves for shoes and bags. Duplicate that in your space so everything has a home.

803. Save time cleaning dirt, mud, and snowy ice left on the floor by shoes and boots. Add a boot tray by the door that is used most often. Not sure where to find a boot tray? Target has a line of organizing products made by California Closets, which offers a few styles of trays, even some with lift top benches. If buying a new piece of furniture is not in your budget or you simply don't have the space, try an aluminum foil baking tray with a lip.

804. Between shoes, backpacks, coats, umbrellas, and mail, the entryway can quickly become a catchall for clutter. If this tends to happen in your house, then you probably don't have designated homes for things. When family members don't know where to put something, they drop it. (Granted, this can also happen when they do know where something belongs, but with a plan, you at least have a better chance.) Try a slim floor-to-ceiling bookshelf on which you can give each family member his or her own shelf. Shoes fit well on the shelves, and hooks can be added to one or both sides of the bookshelf for items like umbrellas and backpacks. Since the entryway is the first thing you see when you arrive home, a neat one sets the tone for organization throughout the house.

805. Shoes are like coats: we can quickly accumulate too many in the entryway. How many shoes do you have sitting in your entryway or shoved in the bottom of the hall closet? Without looking, do you know which pairs they are? If you can't identify them all, then ask yourself if you really need them. It might be better to give the gently used ones to someone without many shoes. Look over the pile of shoes. Do they have a layer of dust on them? Are they still in style? Do they still fit? Try paring down the collection by at least 50 percent.

806. How many coats do you have in your hall closet? If you pack too many coats into a tight space, it makes it virtually impossible to put away the one you are wearing. And since it is so difficult to get them in and out, you'll tend to wear the same one over and over or not put it away at all. Take a few minutes to look at how many coats you have hanging there. Ask yourself if each one is in season, in style, and the right size for the person who wears it. Do you have two coats for the same purpose (like rain-coats)? Asking these questions can help you pare down the collection and move some out, either permanently or until next season.

807. Children's school and camp back-packs need a home. Having them take their bags to their rooms usually does not last, and it actually wastes more time since you end up having to wait while they run to their rooms to get them in the morning. If you are short on space to store the backpacks, try sliding them underneath a bench or storing them in a bench with a lid. The floor of the pantry can sometimes work, as can a hook on the inside of the front hall closet.

808. Recycling is a great thing to do for our environment, but some days it can be a challenge to add that task to your already overloaded schedule. Make recycling easier by adding the pickup dates to your calendar. Have a clear plan for which family member is in charge of which task related to recycling. Keep all the supplies (like scissors and twine for newspapers) handy. And try keeping the recycling cans close to the door so you can collect a small quantity in the kitchen and then easily toss them in the correct can, without going all the way to the back of the garage or down the driveway. If you are responsible for driving the recycling to the collection facility, then be sure to wrap this errand around an already existing habit so you won't forget or put it off. If the recycling center is downtown near the library where you already go every week, then drop the recycling off on the way and let the library trip act as a reward for completing a not-so-fun task.

809. Valuable time can be spent looking for an item in the refrigerator, or worse, shopping for an item you already own. So take a few minutes to organize the inside of the refrigerator and toss all UFOs (Unidentified Food Objects).

810. The freezer is another place where we can lose time looking for things. And you may have an everyday freezer and also a spare oversized one for stock items. Before putting away items that you have packaged yourself, be sure to label them. To make this easier, attach a roll of masking tape and a permanent marker somewhere nearby.

811. If you have ever had a stack of plastic storage containers topple out of the cabinet when you opened it, or if you've had to spend any time at all looking for a matching lid, then you know how challenging storing these containers can be. First, pare down your collection by tossing any containers that do not seal tightly or that are lidless. Then, nest the ones you can, and store the lids on a lid holder on the inside of the cabinet door. If you have an abundance of storage containers, try tucking some in a box in your pantry area or laundry room; as you need more, perhaps to send leftovers home with friends, grab them from there.

812. Label your pantry shelves with the category of what belongs on each shelf. This makes putting items away easier, and it also saves time when you are making out your shopping list.

813. At the start of each month, look over the calendar and make a note of which cards you need to mail out to whom. Sit down and write all the cards out at one time and in the spot where you will place the postage on the envelope, write the date you need to mail the card. To make this even easier, keep a stash of greeting cards on hand for a variety of occasions.

47

Organizing Solutions for Living Space

814. Store all refrigerated sandwich-making items in one plastic caddy so you can pull them all out at once and have everything you need to make a sandwich, instead of digging through the shelves and pulling items out one by one.

815. To avoid having to spend time wiping up sticky spills from marinades, place jars of it in paper muffin cups. That way if they spill, you can just toss out the muffin cup, and you won't have to clean the shelf.

816. Use a condiment caddy. Take a small plastic container and fill it with all the condiments in your refrigerator; then, whenever you need one, simply slide it out and grab what you need.

817. Try a battery organizer to store all your batteries and keep them visible. Battery organizers mount to the wall or inside the cabinet door. They keep various sizes visible, so you'll know what you have at a glance, and many come with battery testers or flashlights attached to them.

818. Save time by organizing your junk drawer. When you need a match, rubber band, or permanent marker, it is easier to be able to open the drawer and see everything instead of having to hunt around. Use box lids or egg cartons as drawer dividers and give each item a spot in the drawer; when you are done using it, put it where it belongs instead of just tossing it in.

819. If you tend to collect plastic shopping bags, place them in a bag organizer for safekeeping. You can buy plastic bag organizers, or you can take an old tote bag and cut a small hole in the bottom so you fill from the top and dispense from the bottom.

820. Trim down the glassware collection in your cabinet. Often, valuable cabinet space is taken up by excess glasses used only on occasion. Reclaim the space by relegating spare glasses to a more difficult-to-reach top shelf or into a box labeled "party ware" and store it away. Use the additional space for items you use on a regular basis.

821. The next time you are on hold on the phone, take the time to check that all the pens and markers in the pen cup or junk drawer work. Grabbing pens that don't write is a waste of time.

822. Tuck a few working pens and scrap paper into a decorative basket or single easy-to-reach drawer, so you won't have to scrounge for it the next time you want to write a note.

IT WORKED FOR HER

"When using a recipe to keep track of when the food item has last been served, I use a pencil and on the back of it write the date [of the] last time it was served. For example, I served Academy Inn Salad Friday, and on the card was a little note that it was last served June of last year."

Rebecca Murphy, KY

823. Set up a drink station with all the items you use to make your favorite drink. If you are a coffee or tea drinker, you might put a mug or two, sugar, tea bags, coffee filters, and so on. If you prefer blended drinks, such as smoothies, then the blender and your glass with straws might go there. Having everything you need within reach makes it easier to prepare the drinks without having to open and close multiple cabinets.

824. If you find yourself wasting tons of time looking for the lid to match the sippy cup or plastic storage container, you are not alone. As an alternative to investing in one of those spin holders that require you to purchase only a certain kind of plastic container, you can hang a lid holder on the inside of your cabinet door. Measure first to be sure the cabinet shelf is back far enough to allow room for the holder to fit. A less expensive option is to hang a small tote bag, and slip the lids in there.

825. Save time unsticking clear wrap from itself by installing an under-the-cabinet wrap dispenser. This allows you to pull just the right amount of clear wrap off the roll without it doubling back on itself.

826.

Instead of opening and closing commonly used spice containers when preparing a meal, place the ones you use most in an auto-dispensing holder that allows you to squeeze the right amount of spice out without having to unscrew a lid. These handy spice containers can be found at organizing and home goods stores.

827.

Inevitably, there is going to be the need for a catchall area in the kitchen. So create one! Try something of a manageable size like a single drawer or a decorative basket. Then make sorting through it part of your weekly routine so it stays a manageable size.

IT WORKED FOR HER

"Though I love cookbooks and read them like novels, I do not like to collect them, as they take up too much space, and it is too time-consuming to search through an entire book for the recipe I want. So whether it is a recipe I clip out, receive from a friend, or [copy] from a book borrowed from the library, I store them in an accordion folder—the kind with pockets listed from A–Z. Appetizers go in A, Beef-type recipes go in B, C=Chicken, D=Desserts, and so on. I use the extra pockets for diet specific needs W=WW [Weight Watchers] recipes, etc."

LuAnn Schafer Bridgewater, NJ

828. Place the items you use each day, like your cell phone, purse, wallet, and keys, in a handy spot and, return them every time you are done using them, so they are there the next time you need them.

829. Give each toy a home, and get everyone in the habit of putting the toys back when done playing with them.

830. Labeling each container, drawer, and shelf makes it quicker to put things away and to locate items when you need them. If your child is too young to read, you can use pictures alongside the words.

831. When storing toys in the playroom, do not use lids on the bins. It is much easier to toss items like stuffed animals and dolls into a bin if there is no lid to be removed first.

832. To avoid lengthy weekend cleanups of playrooms, post playroom rules that everyone agrees with. One toy out at a time per child during playdates or two toys out per child is a good guideline.

833. Give your kids a ten-minute warning to let them know when to clean up, and everything will be put away before you need to leave.

834. If your child is past choking-hazard age, then ziplock bags are a big time-saver. Storing small pieces for toys in these bags makes it much easier to keep track of them. Board game pieces, puzzle pieces, doll accessories, and many other items are easy to find when contained in a see-through ziplock bag.

835. Stop picking up little toy pieces and crafts parts that should be used only under adult supervision by storing adult-supervised-only toys up high, out of the reach of little fingers. That way there is no chance of your finding hundreds of beads, foam pieces, or other messy items scattered around that take lots of time to pick up and sort.

836. Save time by using a hanger organizer to store extra hangers—especially wire hangers from the dry cleaner. Don't waste another minute with tangled nests of wire hangers.

48.

Organizing Solutions for Storage Space

837. Store out-of-season clothing outside your everyday wardrobe closet. Keep similar garments together in small bins instead of opting for the oversized storage tubs. This allows you to pull out just what you need as the seasons change instead of living out of one huge tub for several months. And don't forget to label the bins. (Warning: Many of the plastic storage bags that deflate and scrunch items inside have been known to leave a lasting chemical smell on the items left inside, so it is suggested that you try them out first.)

838. If you are saving clothing for younger siblings to grow into, store them in bins clearly labeled with the size; be sure to store similar sizes together. Do not put away anything that is in need of repair or stain removal; handle repairs before you store items away.

839. Hyloft is just one of the products available today to add storage space to your garage. The shelving unit hangs from the ceiling, giving you a loft to store items. Warning: Measure first to be sure that your cars will fit underneath it once it is installed.

840. When adding shelving units to your garage, take an extra moment to measure by pulling your car into the garage and opening all the doors. Mark where the doors open out to; that way you will not place storage too close to the car, obstructing your ability to get in and out of the car and to open and close the cabinets.

841. When organizing your tool area, put together a small box with the most commonly needed items like a tape measure, screwdrivers, flashlight, level, and so on. That way, when you need one of those items for a small project like hanging a piece of artwork, you will not have to sort through your entire tool set.

842. When placing items in storage areas like the attic, garage, and basement, take an extra moment to store them off the floor and near similar items (like with like!) to make them easy to find. Storing items up off the floor is important for many reasons, including avoiding water damage and infestation of little critters. (You can purchase an item called a bin warehouse. This shelving unit is made up of cubbies so you can slide one bin in per cubby. This means no stacking, so items won't crush; plus, it is a breeze to pull out the one bin you need without stacking and un-stacking all of them.)

843. Be aware of the humidity and dryness levels in the storage areas. For example, you would not want to store precious photographs where they will be too moist or become brittle. If you need a dehumidifier, it can make the difference between your stored treasures lasting a lifetime or being ruined.

844. When you are deciding how to organize a closet, especially a wardrobe closet, try doing it by function. If you hang all the fancy dresses together, they will be easy to look through when you need one. The same is true for your other clothing items, like jeans.

845. Store clothing that is not your current size somewhere else, if you keep it at all. First of all, you don't need to be reminded all the time that they do not fit you. Second, they take valuable closet space away from the clothes you do wear and love.

846. Do not be restricted by dressers and hanging bars. If your clothing folds better than it hangs or you are not a fan of hangers, then opt for cubbies in the closet instead of a hanging bar. Dresser drawers are not always the best choice, since it is difficult to see what you have and things can easily become unfolded. If you love to hang your items, then move the bar up higher and add a second bar below it for twice the hanging space.

HAVE MORE TIME TODAY!

1. Think of one thing you misplace almost every day, and give it a new home so you can find it when you need it.
2. Get everyone in the house involved by deciding on a new family rule that will help keep the living areas clutter-free.
3. Work on one of the storage areas in your home (like a closet or garage) a little bit at a time until you get it how you want it.

TRY THIS:

Have everyone in the house pitch in for a five minute tidy-up at the end of the evening; you can make it more fun by playing a song or setting a timer and making it a contest.

REPEAT AFTER ME:

"Love it or lose it."

Part Seventeen:

Special Times and Stressful Ones

There are times when you have to add tasks to your already-full daily to-do list, whether to plan a party or remodel a room. Special times do not have to be stressful times, though. Here's how to balance it all without falling behind.

49.

Holidays and Birthdays

847. Themed gifts make gift-giving easy. Once you hone in on a theme, you narrow down your search for the perfect gift. Maybe one year you can plan to give everyone arts-and-crafts gifts, and in following years opt for books or board games. That means for every birthday party and holiday, you can plan on one-stop shopping.

848. Shopping in advance becomes much easier when you choose a "theme of the year," since you can shop in bulk right after the holidays to take advantage of the post-holiday sales and keep a stock of gifts on hand to use all year long.

849. If you will not be seeing the birthday person but plan to ship a gift to him or her, try shopping online or at a store that offers direct shipping direct to the person. This saves you time since you do not have to repack the item and take it to a shipping location.

850. Remember to keep it simple. The important thing is the time you spend celebrating, not how your party measures up to the one you or your child attended last week. If you don't want to have fireworks or a blow-up ball pit, don't. Everyone just wants to have fun, so don't spend time overdoing!

851. Save time by sending out email versions of invitations instead of paper versions. There are many online sites (www.evite.com, for example) that offer a wide variety at no charge. Choose from many themes and customize your invitation.

852. Having a children's birthday party? As you prepare the day before, take a moment to scoop ice cream into a muffin tin lined with foil muffin liners, and then cover with clear wrap. Keep it in the freezer until serving time. Each child will have his or her own individually-sized portion, and you won't have to wrestle with the scooper and melting ice cream on the big day.

TEN STEPS TO PLANNING A PARTY

1. Choose a theme.
2. Plan your budget.
3. Write your guest list.
4. Determine a location.
5. Send the invitations.
6. Shop for the decorations.
7. Pick the entertainment.
8. Locate friends/family to help.
9. Choose the food and cake.
10. Send thank-you cards.

IT WORKED FOR HER

"Keep an ear open to family and friends that you buy for (holidays, birthdays, etc.). When they mention something, put it in an "Others" shopping log. This way, when you need to purchase something for them, you can go right to your log and see what they want. I find that Excel is great software for these logs. You can organize things into categories, sort things when you need to, etc. Plus, when you type a website in, you can click on that reference and go straight to the website (saving you time!). You can also print these lists and keep them in your organizer. When you are out shopping and you need to buy a gift for someone, you can look at your list. Or, if you see something that is on your list, you can compare prices to see if the place you have logged is less expensive than what you are seeing in the store."

Amy Stanley Greensburg, PA

853. Plan an undecorating party to make the process go faster and be more enjoyable. This can become a new family tradition. Don't forget to spend a little time packing carefully and labeling the boxes, so you can save time next year when you pull the decorations out again.

854. If the few weeks of holidays go by too fast and you need more time to celebrate and see everyone, extend the holiday season into January so you are not so rushed. Having family get-togethers with extended family or close friends after the New Year is a great way to enjoy spending time with loved ones when you are not on a tight timetable.

855. Host an open house. This allows friends and family to pop by during the open house hours and eliminates the need for you to try to find time to go to each of their homes separately.

856. Create a gift-wrapping station where you store all the wrapping paper, gift bags, and boxes. Having all the supplies in one location makes gift-wrapping easier.

857. Set up a gift-wrapping caddy. Take a single bucket, basket, or box and fill it with all the necessary supplies, like scissors and tape; that way, you will have all the supplies on hand when needed and in a handy, portable carrying case in the event you choose to wrap in another location.

858. Store bows, tags, and embellishments in one place. To avoid ribbons tangling, take an over-the-door clear, plastic shoe holder and hang it in the wrapping area. Place one type of ribbon in each slot, punch a small hole, and thread the ribbon through.

859. Multitask by opting to host a gift-wrapping party. Invite friends, socialize, and share gift-wrapping ideas while you work; this can also get you away from the prying eyes of your family as you try to wrap.

860. Avoid procrastinating about writing out your holiday cards by breaking up the large task into mini-tasks. Simply divide the number of cards you are choosing to send by the number of days you have left to mail them. That way you know how many you need to write out per day and can avoid hours of writing in one sitting. (Don't forget that card-writing is a portable task. Pop a few in your task tote bag, and carry them with you when you leave the house. As long as you have a flat surface, you can write out a few while waiting for your child to come out of school, for a meeting to begin, or while sitting in your physician's waiting room.

861. Try putting your holiday card list in a spreadsheet and printing the addresses directly on the envelopes to save time. You can print in festive colors and even opt to add a holiday-themed logo.

862. Avoid the stress of getting everyone together for a family portrait. Instead, create a unique and memorable holiday card by collecting various photographs from the past year, along with your children's artwork and other treasures. Then arrange them on paper and make color photocopies to send as the card.

863. If you still prefer to get a family holiday portrait taken, then try to get the photo done over the summer when there are much shorter lines. Remember, you do not have to send a classic holiday photo—you can send a casual photo taken on your family vacation or something else fun.

864. Get the whole family involved in stuffing holiday cards by setting up an assembly line. Children can add a fun touch to the envelope, while someone else sticks on the stamps.

865. Instead of buying gifts for everyone in the family, you can suggest a new tradition of putting everyone's name in a hat and picking a person to buy for. If just buying one gift is not enjoyment enough, you can put the names back in the hat and each person can pick a second name.

866. Instead of attempting to make a dozen types of cookies, invite friends and family to a cookie swap. Have each person bake one dozen cookies (each person bakes a different kind). Each participant brings a cookie tin to be filled and then meets up with or picks up the cookies from the other people.

867. Make a holiday binder using a one-inch, three-ring binder filled with three-hole punched sheet protectors, lined filler paper, and a three-hole punched pencil pouch. Use the binder for brainstorming menu ideas, guest lists, shopping lists, gift ideas, and more. Then slip ideas clipped from catalogs, receipts, recipes, and more into the sheet protectors. Keep pens in the pouch, and store the binder away with Halloween decorations so you can pull it out and use it again in plenty of time next year.

868. Book baby-sitters well ahead of time for adult-only holiday celebrations and for shopping time. It is a busy time of year, so it is important to reserve their time *early*.

869. Before your calendar is filled up with obligations and other requirements, block out time for the fun stuff, including time to do nothing at all. This is vital to enjoying the season.

870. Forget "perfect." If you try to live up to your own impossible standards over the holiday season, you will take a lot of the enjoyment out of it. Instead of spending time finding the perfect gift, tying the perfect bow, and decorating the perfect gingerbread man cookie, opt to go for "good" and ignore the imperfections.

871. Deciding in advance how many events you and your family want to attend will be a huge time- and stress-saver. Once you have a number to accept, then you can look at the options and choose that number, instead of debating about each and every new invitation or overburdening your schedule by accepting all of them.

872. Be sure to schedule some downtime after the holiday season so that once the madness passes, you will have some time to recoup. Schedule this time in advance so that it is already booked, and you don't run the risk of over-booking your time.

873. Buying gifts in bulk and then sepa-rating the items into gift baskets allows you to customize gifts for friends and fam-ily while saving time, since you can make fewer trips to the store.

874. Once you have your home decorated the way you like it, take a picture of the decorations so next year you remember how things were set up. It is also helpful to mark things like garlands using twist ties to note the points to tack them up, so they hang how you want them to.

875. Clearly label the boxes of decorations so you can save time looking for items in boxes next year. Pack similar decorations together, and mark which boxes need to be brought out first.

876. Pack away holiday gift wrap, holiday sweaters, and other seasonal items that do not need to be left out year-round.

877. Whenever possible, save time by going semi-homemade with food preparations, wrapping, and decorations. Instead of making a lighted garland, buy the lights and garland and twist them together; or, instead of making a pumpkin pie, buy one and add dollops of vanilla-extract-infused whipped topping and pecans.

SEVEN STEPS AND TWENTY MINUTES TO A HOUSE YOU CAN ENTERTAIN IN

878. Gather up cleaning supplies in a bucket or laundry basket to tote around with you. Here are some items to toss in your cleaning kit:
• Duster cloths
• Premoistened cleaning solution wipes
• An extension cord for the vacuum
• Garbage bags
• A lint roller

879. Shake doormats outside the door guests will use, and sweep the walkway.

880. Wipe the glass in the front door, the windows at eye level, and any tabletop picture frames guests may handle.

881. Clean the refrigerator handle and kitchen cabinet drawer pulls.

882. Freshen the bathroom surfaces with handy cleaning wipes, swish the toilet, and refill paper products.

883. Spot-mop the floors, and run the vacuum on high-traffic areas only.

884. Lint roll the couches and chairs where pets often sit.

50.
Moving, Travel, and Vacation

885. Ask your realtor if his or her office offers a concierge service through which someone can handle the transfer of all your utilities and other details. Being able to delegate that is a huge time-saver. If you can't delegate the job, you can at least make it easier by making whatever transfers you can online. Most utility companies offer this option; simply visit their websites to find out.

886. Change your mailing address online at www.usps.com, and have your mail forwarded without having to make a time-consuming stop at the post office.

887. Keep track of your move by making a moving notebook. Take a one-inch, three-ring binder and add some sheet protectors, index tabs, folders, and notepaper. Carry this with you all the time. This is where you can store your lists of things to do, business cards, important numbers, contracts, and so much more. No more hunting for lost papers!

888. Take this opportunity to pare down to what you use and love. You may think that you'll go through your stuff after the move, but that is rarely the case. Usually the boxes of "junk" sit in the garage or basement for years. Don't spend time packing or money moving stuff you don't really need. For example, do you need to move three egg separators? Or can you part with two of them? If you locate a charity to donate to, it can make parting with the items easier.

889. Choose a charity that picks up. Keep their number in your moving note-book. Call them often, do not wait until you have *everything* to give them in one shot, have them come and take away all the stuff that is still good but that you do not need any longer. Giving the items to charity is a better use of your time than planning and hosting a garage sale before you leave. You'd most likely have leftover stuff anyway, and the sale would take time away from preparing to move.

890. Consider having a moving party. Invite friends and family to bring boxes. You supply the pizza, put on music, and pack the night away. This can be a great use of your time, since you can socialize and create fond memories before you leave.

891. Pack like items with like items. Make the boxes manageable in size and weight; paper is heavier than you think! A heavier box takes more time to move than two smaller boxes, and the larger boxes are much safer, since you can injure yourself trying to carry a heavy box.

892. Save time packing and unpacking by labeling everything! And label all sides of boxes including the lid. You might even try color-coding. For most of us, our mind processes shapes and colors faster than words, so by marking each kitchen box with a red circle and each living room box with blue triangle and so on, you can unload the moving van faster. Post a sign in the doorway of each room that corresponds with the boxes. This is especially helpful because when rooms are empty, it can be difficult to know which room is which. This takes the guesswork out of the process, and you'll have to answer fewer questions like, "Which room does this box go in?"

893. Avoid having to waste time running to the store just to buy essentials or digging through boxes to find something on moving day. Pack a bag of the essentials, so when you get to the new house, you do not have to open boxes to find toilet paper or a cup. Include bath towels, paper products, glasses, sheets, and any medication or vitamins.

894. Packing is stressful enough; don't waste time by pressuring yourself to make decisions about whether or not to keep something that you are really unsure about or that may or may not work in the new space. If you know you don't need it, give it away or throw it out. But if you're not certain, create a "maybe" box. Pack up all the items you might or might not be able to use in the new space. Take them with you to your new place, and once you are moved in, if you don't unpack that box in six months, let the box go. (Warning: Do not open the box! If you do, you will only be reminded of all the reasons why you thought you needed to hold onto the items, and you'll hang onto the stuff even longer.)

895. When flying, be sure not to pack prohibited items. This will help you avoid lengthy delays at check-in. To view a complete list of what is prohibited, visit the Transportation Security Administration (TSA) website at www.tsa.gov.

896. When traveling by airplane, leave gifts unwrapped to allow for easy inspection. Otherwise they may be unwrapped by security, and you'll have to spend time rewrapping them. (Consider mailing the gifts to where you are traveling before you leave.)

897. Save time cleaning dirt off your packed clothes by slipping your shoes into plastic bags before packing them.

898. If you have to go through a metal detector to board an airplane, train, or bus, avoid wearing clothing, jewelry, and accessories that contain metal. Metal items will most likely set off the alarm on the metal detector, delaying your check-in. Instead, put metal *inside* your carry-on bag. This includes jewelry, spare change in your pocket, cell phones, and Blackberries.

IT WORKED FOR HER

"Whenever I travel, when folding clothes, I lay a piece of tissue paper in the creases of clothing that tend to wrinkle. When I unpack it, there are no wrinkles, and that means no ironing! What a time-saver. And instead of buying new tissue paper, I save the stuff I get in gifts."

Lee C. Edison, NJ

899. Whenever your luggage will be screened, don't pack undeveloped film or cameras with film still inside. The baggage-screening equipment may damage undeveloped film, most likely erasing all the photographs. The same is true of many computer CDs and other recorded material.

900. Clearly understand the policies for your mode of transportation. For example, for flying, carry-on baggage is limited to one carry-on bag plus one personal item. Personal items include laptop computers, diaper bags, or camera cases—no exceptions. Avoid lengthy debates and repacking by bringing only what you know you are allowed to bring.

901. Have directions written out, along with the actual address of your destination and a phone number that will get you the answers you need at the time of day you are traveling. No sense having a phone number for your booking agent if his or her office will not be open that day; instead, you need an emergency phone number.

902. Place identification tags *in and on* each piece of your luggage. Another time-saving tip is to take a photo of your luggage; that way, if it is misplaced, it can easily be identified.

903. Save time searching the luggage carousel for your bags, which these days probably look very similar to all the other bags. Tie a brightly colored ribbon or scrap of material to the handle so you can easily differentiate yours from the sea of bags.

904. Try to avoid bringing food or drink to security checkpoints. You'll only hold up the process. Additionally, you will most likely be asked to discard the item or be asked to consume it prior to stepping through the checkpoint.

905. Easily put a hold on your mail delivery by visiting www.usps.com. Often, you can place your newspapers on hold online as well; and if you know you'll fall behind reading your mail, you might opt to pause magazine subscriptions to give yourself time to catch up.

906. Let that vacation mode linger a little longer once you get home by creating a plan to catch up on the laundry. You might consider a short trip to your local Laundromat, so you can do all the loads at one time. Or you might reserve a little money from your vacation budget and opt for the Laundromat's wash and dry service; you drop it off and pick it up once it is folded.

51.
Household Repairs, Remodeling, and DIY

907. Repair broken things in your home when they are still minor, *before* they become major issues. Waiting longer just makes the repair cost more time and money.

908. Does it make sense for you to do it? Sometimes a do-it-yourself (DIY) project ends up costing you more than if you left the project to the professionals. Between the tools you need to buy or rent, the supplies you need to purchase, and the time it takes you to learn, you may be better off leaving the project to someone else more experienced.

909. To determine whether a project is worth your time and effort, follow this calculation: if you make $45,000 a year, your salary including benefits equals out to a little over $30 an hour. Professionals can complete most jobs you'd consider doing yourself for less than your hourly wage when you add up how many hours it would take you to learn, then do it without (you hope) making any errors. All this means that you can earn in just a few hours or less what it will cost you to have someone else clean the house or do yard work. Professionals come with the supplies, and they know the best way to get the job done. Plus, since they do it for a living, they probably like doing the job much more than you would. Additionally, they have insurance should something go awry, and often, doing it yourself invalidates the manufacturer's warranty.

910. Mistakes cost you both time and money. The bigger the mistake, the more time and money it will take to fix it. Plus, if you can't finish the job and need to call in a professional, you can expect to pay 10 to 30 percent more for them to redo the work.

911. If you don't love the idea of doing the task, then you will put it off. We tend to procrastinate about things we don't think we will enjoy. The time you waste thinking about and preparing for the task, but not *doing* it, is time you could have spent doing something else.

912. Consider opting for delivery when you make a large purchase. It might seem like the fee is high, but consider these questions: Is your vehicle large enough to transport the item? If not, how much will it cost you to rent a truck? Do you void any warranties by carrying the item home yourself? (If it breaks in transit, you are usually responsible.) Have you measured to be sure it will fit through the doorways and hallways? If they deliver, they remove the packaging, which can cost you extra to have disposed. (Often the delivery charge is negotiable; it never hurts to ask.)

913. If the store offers an option to assemble the item for you, consider taking advantage of that offer. They know how to build it, and if they make an error they are responsible. If you make a mistake, you might end up having to buy another one.

914. When considering whether or not to do a project yourself, do not overestimate your skill set. You are capable of lots of things, but is this one of them? Do you have the skills, energy, and desire?

915. Do you own all the *correct* tools for the job? If not, can you rent them at a reasonable rate? If you'll need to rent, be sure to call ahead and reserve.

916. Think about your deadline. If you need it done by a certain time, can you complete the job by then? Remember that you should estimate a project to take 30 percent longer than you expect.

917. Ask yourself if you can dispose of the waste safely. Lead-based paint, car tires, and motor oil are considered hazardous waste and can be costly and time-consuming to dispose of; when a professional completes the job, part of the pricing includes waste removal.

918. Ask yourself if you can do the job safely. For example, do you need help moving something large or heavy, or will you be on a ladder and need a spotter? If you need help, have you identified someone who can help you? If you overextend yourself, it takes you longer to do the job. Plus, you run the risk of injury, which is no time-saver at all.

919. Does the project require permits? If so, can you get them, and how much time and money will they cost you? Usually the professionals include the permits in their estimates.

920. A major mistake is thinking that you can do the job better. Sometimes you can, but often someone else can do a comparable or better job. Don't let your ego rule.

921. Sometimes, although it makes more sense to hire someone, it is just not in your budget. If this is the case, consider negotiating the fees or reviewing your budget to see where you can cut a little for a month or two so you can find the money. It may be worth it to free up the time you would have to spend doing the job yourself.

922. It does not always have to come down to hiring someone outright. You might have a friend or neighbor who is skilled in that area and is willing to walk you through it. Or you can barter with someone by offering your skills in exchange for his or hers. Lastly, you might be able to locate a local college student who could be your extra pair of hands on the job.

HAVE MORE TIME TODAY!

1. Choose a theme for this year's gifts to make gift-giving easier and more enjoyable.

2. Save time planning your next day-trip or vacation by storing all the paperwork related to the trip in a single location and setting up a packing station when you are preparing to leave.

3. Pick a day this week to catch up on a few minor household repairs, like changing a washer on the faucet or replacing a light bulb, before they become time-consuming emergencies.

TRY THIS:

Create a file to hold all the papers related to an upcoming event, like a move, a party you are planning, or a vacation. Be sure to label the file clearly, and always put it back in the same spot so you can find it again.

REPEAT AFTER ME:

"Our family enjoys the simple pleasures of the holidays."

Part Eighteen:

Enjoy Newfound Time

You've done it! You have officially come to the end of the book, which means that you now have a plan to take back your time! There is just one more thing I need to mention. Now that you are using systems and routines that allow you more time in your day, we need to be sure that these stay in place. You've done the hard work; we want to be sure that you can enjoy your newfound time and that you don't allow yourself to slide back into old time-wasting habits.

52.

Remember That the Little Stuff Makes a Big Difference

923. Keep your eyeglasses or sunglasses on a decorative eyeglass pin that you can wear, so you'll always know where you glasses are. To see examples of the pins, visit www.jamienovak.com.

924. Fix it. Tasks take longer when the items you need to complete the task are not fully functional. For example, does your cordless phone die often because it needs a new battery? Does vacuuming take longer because the filter needs to be cleaned?

925. Upgrade! Is your technology slow and wasting your time? Slow printer, weak vacuum, inefficient washer? Upgrade!

926. Color-code your keys by adding a key identifier to them. This makes it easier to identify them quickly. Also, to identify buttons on a keypad faster, add a dot of color using a permanent marker or nail polish; a dot of red for off and a dot of green for on makes it easy to see which key to push to turn on and off the phone, fan, or other items.

927. Choose to order your prescriptions via mail order through your medical insurance. Not only will you not have to wait in line at the pharmacy, but they often cost less as well.

928. Try using a buff-colored nail polish on your nails. Dark colors show chips faster; you can save time if your manicure lasts longer.

929. Save time picking out what to wear by buying pieces that coordinate with one another. A few basic clothing items that all mix and match can save you lots of time.

930. Save time trying to discern black from navy by hanging navy clothing on a specially marked hanger. A twist tie around the neck of the hanger works well.

931. Choose no-iron, machine-washable, easy-care clothing. You'll spend less time and money by not running back and forth to the dry cleaner and not ironing.

932. Eighteen minutes more. When you are working on an area, go for just eighteen minutes more. For example, after cleaning one room, while you still have the supplies out, go for just eighteen minutes more in another room. Then, when your time is up, be sure to stop, since going over by too much can throw off your schedule.

933. If you waste time searching for your wallet in the bottom of your purse, use a red or bright-colored wallet so you can spot it easily.

934. Stop wasting time transferring items from one purse to another. Instead, use a purse organizer; fill the organizer with what you need, and simply pull it out and slip it in whichever purse you plan to use that day. You can see examples of the interior purse organizers at www.jamienovak.com.

935. Designate one spot in the house for items to pack for vacation, sell at a garage sale, return, mail, and so on. Keeping like items together makes life easier.

936. Carry a list of things to buy according to store. Without a list, you are more likely to forget things, and that means extra trips.

937. Stop wasting time looking for receipts and other papers in the bottom of your purse, in your overstuffed wallet, or in your briefcase. Instead, tuck a small, plastic envelope with a Velcro closure in your bag, and take that extra moment when you are handed a receipt to slip it into the envelope.

938. Leave a container of touch-up cleaning wipes in rooms like the bathroom and kitchen. That way you can save time by touching up here and there, instead of a doing a deep clean each time.

939. Clean the shower while you are taking one. Saves time and water!

940. Frequent stores that offer pick up and delivery services. Things like renting movies, buying stamps, and getting your dry cleaning done are all less time-consuming when you can opt for pick up and/or delivery.

941. Keep a stash of hostess gifts on hand to grab last-minute when you are invited to an event. A few generic gifts such as candles, decorative wine bags, and centerpieces can save you time when you are rushing out the door and don't have time to stop to pick something up. (Keeping these items on hand helps your wallet, too, since stopping at convenience stores for these items usually adds to the price.)

942. When you need to buy a part and you are not exactly sure what it is called or where it is kept in the store, take a photo of the item with you when you go shopping. Snapping a quick picture of a pipefitting or cable connector beforehand can save you time looking around the store or having to return a wrong purchase. With a picture to refer to, a salesperson is better able to assist you.

943. Remember that when you don't know what to do, you will tend to do nothing at all. So instead of sitting around wondering what the next step is to complete a task, do a little research. Once you find someone who can offer the next step, you will stop wasting time with trial and error or procrastinating.

944. When you need to do a task for the first time, find someone who has already done it, and take notes from that person. For example, say you are now in charge of creating the newsletter for your organization. You can either start from scratch or check with the person who did the job before you to see what tips he or she has and ask if he or she has a template you can use. There's no sense in reinventing the wheel.

945. Signs you are overcommitted and stressed-out because of it are unexplained bruises, bumping into things, the inability to remember where you put things like your keys, misplacing things, talking to yourself (more than usual), trouble sleeping or trouble staying asleep, inability to recall events that happened only hours or days ago (like what you had for breakfast), and a feeling that your days all blend together and you have trouble distinguishing between them.

946. Getting and giving consumable gifts saves everyone time. When you ask for consumable gifts, like tickets to a play, a day at the spa, or dinner, you will not receive an actual item that requires care. And when you choose to give consumable gifts, it saves time spent shopping and deciding what to buy.

53.

Start and Finish Your Days on the Right Note

947. Progressive alarm clocks are a great choice. Instead of a single, loud buzz startling you awake, these alarms chime softly at first. The chime increases in frequency and intensity as your wake-up time approaches, so you awaken much more naturally, eliminating the need for a snooze button.

948. Snooze buttons are dangerous. The thought of "just a minute longer" can be too tempting to pass up. And that minute can set your morning routine back by a lot. Try plugging in your alarm clock across the room, so you will actually have to get out of bed to turn it off. Once you are up, don't allow yourself to go back to bed.

949. Preparing the evening before for the next day is a powerful way to take charge and get more done. At some point during the evening, check your calendar for the next day, write a to-do list, and gather the items you'll need. For example, if rain is in the forecast, you can grab your umbrella now, locate your cell phone and charge it, and set out your clothes.

950. Wrap up at the end of the day by putting away projects you were working on, whether or not you finished them. Put things away, clean up, and leave your home and office better than you found it that morning.

951. If you tend to walk out of the house without things like your lunch, then try the over-the-doorknob reminder. These notepads are specially designed to fit over the doorknob and allow you to jot down notes like "grab lunch." Since the doorknob is the last thing you touch on the way out the door, if you've forgotten the item, the note will remind you. (Note: Pictures of the over-the-doorknob reminders can be seen at www.jamienovak.com.)

952. Leave time to tidy up at the end of the day. These quick pickups will only need to take five to ten minutes daily, but they will save you a ton of time since you'll avoid a huge mess piling up that requires a full day to clean up.

953. At the end of the day, pull out what you need for the next day. If you plan to work on a file at work, pull it out and leave it on your desk or chair. If you plan to make a phone call to the credit card company, pull out your statement and put it on the kitchen counter. Or if you plan to return library books, pull them out and put them on the front seat of your car. Whatever you plan to do will take less time if you already have the items ready to go, so prepare in advance.

954. Put away what you are done with for the day *even if* you are not finished yet and plan to get back to it. Sometimes you might not get back to a project as quickly as you anticipated, so the items can get lost, causing you to waste time looking for them again when you need them or distracting you by catching your eye when you're trying to focus on something else.

955. End the work part of the day by transitioning into the evening, whether you are coming back from a job outside your home or not. Try playing soothing music instead of having the television on; change your clothes and (if you wear it) wash off your makeup. Another great idea is to have healthy munchies available as an appetizer to ward off hunger pangs and cranky kids as dinner is cooking.

956. While you are trying out any new morning or evening routine, it can be helpful to post a short checklist in a visible spot so you'll remember your new routine. After about twenty-one days, the new routine will simply be a habit, and you can remove the checklist.

957. Save time during the morning routine by choosing your outfits the night before. (Save even more time by choosing a week's worth of outfits on Sunday; check the weather report, too, so you won't have to waste time picking a new outfit when you wake up to a rainy day you weren't expecting.)

958. Allow your child(ren) to dress themselves. In order to spend less time debating over whether or not they can wear their Halloween costume to school, remove everything from the closet or dresser drawers that is not appropriate.

959. Pack in the evening so you can spend less time in the morning getting ready for school. Tasks always take longer in the morning; do whatever you can at night. Be sure backpacks are packed before bedtime. Along with the backpack, set out everything else needed for the next day, such as scouting uniforms, musical instruments, or sporting equipment.

960. To give yourself more time in the mornings to concentrate on getting each child ready, try staggering their wake-up times. Even an extra five minutes with one child before the other gets up can give you some much needed uninterrupted time.

961. Morning checklists can save everyone time. By writing out what needs to get done on a sheet of paper, your child(ren) can easily see what needs to be done on that day. If your children do not read yet, use pictures for the tasks like a toothbrush, a hairbrush, and a backpack. (No need to rewrite a new checklist for every day; just make one out for the week so that activities specific to a certain day can be noted.)

962. If you volunteer as a class mom, scouting leader, or sports coach, you are bound to have multiple papers you need to keep track of. Save time by placing them in a travel file box that you keep in the back of your car. When you are at the event, you'll have the name and address rosters and all other associated paperwork on hand. Then you can easily carry it into the house if you ever need to.

963. If you find yourself continuously being interrupted by family members asking you to help them with things you want them to be able to do alone, then make a change. For example, if younger children ask you to get the juice boxes for them from the top shelf of the refrigerator, move them to where they can reach them so they stop interrupting you.

964. Hang a master checklist to be sure you and everyone in the home have everything you need before you leave the house. The checklist is best placed near the door you use to leave the house or near the kitchen. Next to the checklist, it might help save time to hang a clear, plastic shoe holder over a door in which you can keep commonly used items like sunglasses, keys, and items that need to leave with you, like mail and library books. Having these items on hand saves valuable time.

965. Preset the table for breakfast. For quick and easy cleanup on rushed days, use paper products. Ease the weekday morning rush by setting the table for breakfast before you go to bed. Put out cereal boxes, sweeteners, and other nonperishable items. Prepare the coffeemaker and set the timer.

966. Give yourself enough time to wake up and get ready *before* the children get up; that way you can give them your full attention, and you'll be less stressed since you'll already be set to go.

967. Make it a family rule that there is no television-watching while getting ready to leave the house. Once *everyone* is ready to walk out the door, *if* there is extra time, then you can turn on the television.

968. With all the commitments family members have, it is imperative to reserve family time before all the spare time is eaten up. Be sure to reserve one evening a week free from outside activities. To ensure this happens, block that night off on the calendar at the start of every month, or before you know it, all the evenings will be committed.

969. Try a blackout night once a month. This is when you will pretend that a storm knocked out the power to your home and there is a blackout. Eating by candlelight, playing board games as a family instead of playing computer games alone, no phones, no computers— you'll be amazed at how long the night seems. All the things that plug in or operate on batteries suck valuable time out of our days. They do serve a purpose, but once in a while, it's nice to unplug.

970. Schedule time to work on homework. Without a schedule, homework can be left to the last minute, and then bedtimes are pushed back as the work is squeezed in, causing kids to stay up late and making mornings tough. (Adjust the homework time to fit your child's prime time. Some children need a snack after school before they can work; others do their best work after a few hours off from school, so after dinner might make more sense.)

971. Designating different color tote bags, one for each activity or project, can be a huge time-saver. Instead of packing and repacking bags to carry all the necessary items for that activity, make one bag for each, and just grab the one(s) you need. (Wondering where to store all these bags? Benches with a lift-up seat in the entryway or an oversized, decorative basket are options. Sometimes you can even leave them in the trunk of the car.)

972. Have a look at the calendar in the evening, and have each person list what he or she has planned for the next day; this way, everyone knows where everyone else will be, and you can catch conflicts before it is too late to make an adjustment in the plan.

973.

Try your best to stick to morning and evening routines. The more you practice them, the better you will get. Your morning routine should include getting out the door with everything you need and a clear plan for the day, and the evening routine should include a quick tidying of the rooms, preparing for the next day, and enough time to wind down before bed.

54.

Maintaining Your New Habits and Enjoying Your Newfound Time

974. Focus on your successes instead of what is left undone. There will always be more to do, so if you focus on the undone instead of the completed, you will always feel behind.

975. A very important component to being able to maintain your new habits is to leave enough time to recharge your battery by fitting in downtime and time off to do the fun stuff. The key is to balance work with play.

976. Don't work too hard. If you are all work and you just focus on ticking tasks off your to-do list, you will become bored quickly and resist keeping up your new routines.

977. Review your plan at least once a year with your family. Although you may feel things are going along just fine, those you live with may have a different take on the situation, so ask.

978. Remember that matching your time to meet your priorities is of the utmost importance. Be sure to revamp your goals, and then adjust your schedule to match. Without the desire to spend time on things that are important to you, managing your time well does not seem all that important.

979. Update your plan and make any necessary changes as your life changes. Life will not stay the same, so your time-management systems shouldn't stay the same, or they run the risk of becoming outdated.

980. Mix up the new routines to keep them fresh. Doing the same thing day in and day out can become monotonous, so change things up to keep it interesting.

981. Reward yourself for a job well-done. Whenever you get through a particularly challenging day or make a tough decision, like stepping off a volunteer project you once agreed to, take a moment to do something nice for yourself in return.

982. You can become so accustomed to accomplishing so much more than you used to that you forget how far you have come. Be sure to acknowledge the changes you have made. It can be difficult to remember how challenging getting through the day once was, so always keep in mind just how far you've come.

983. Make adjustments, as needed. No one plan is perfect, so continue doing what is working and try out new ideas if something is not working well. No sense in trying to force yourself into a system that is not right for you. Instead, work with your own style and personality to find the best time-management systems for you.

984. Allow yourself some flexibility with your new plan. It is possible that you won't get it exactly right the first time and you may need to make changes. If that happens, keep in mind that it does not mean you have failed; it simply means you've eliminated one way that will not work, and you get to try again.

985. Don't get discouraged. It takes about twenty-one days to create a new habit. So, if you are trying a new routine and in a week you miss a day, don't give up. Just start again and sooner than you think, it will become a habit, and you won't have to constantly remind yourself to do it.

986. Hang up a few reminders of why you are determined to gain control over your time. You might tack up a photo of your children, your spouse, a relaxing scene like a beach, your blood pressure numbers from your physician, or some other picture that will be a continuous reminder of why time management is important to you. Keep these pictures in a spot where you will see them daily, like in your calendar, on your refrigerator door, or next to your bathroom mirror.

987. Post notes around the house—by the phone or on your calendar—if they will help you remember your new guidelines for managing time. You won't need to keep these notes up forever—just until you are in the new habit.

988. Expect that things will get tough. There is no magic fix, so it's best not to expect that if you implement a few new guidelines, all your time troubles will be history. Set realistic expectations, and when things get tough, remind yourself that you have a plan and this time crunch will pass.

989. Have a plan for how you will regroup when things get tense. When you are able to recognize a need for clarity and perspective, you can step away from the situation and come back when you have a clearer head. Many people report scrubbing the sink, taking a shower, going for a walk, writing out a list, or playing with their child or pet can really help.

990. Allow yourself more time initially to get the new system down. In the beginning, it can take extra time to use a time-management strategy, but that is temporary. Once you get it down, it saves you time, so stick with the new plan.

991. No one can sit and watch a movie with your child like you can; no one can take an evening walk with your spouse like you can. Be sure to continue to strike a balance. You don't want to look back and realize that all the little moments that passed you by while you were planning life were actually the biggest and best parts of your life. Treasure every moment whether it is stressful or calm.

992. The old cliché, "Live each day as if it were your last," can feel a little too dramatic for everyday living. That being said, try your best to live without regrets.

993. The inbox will never be empty, and there will always be more to do. Remember that this is a process, not a destination. If you plan to be happy once you are all caught up, you'll be waiting a long, long time. Instead enjoy the day.

994. Enjoy the feeling of being on top of your schedule, and don't fall prey to the thought that this newfound feeling of control and freedom is too good to last. Once you have your new systems in place, that freedom and control is your new life. Will there be days when things are a little rocky? Sure, but that is temporary.

995. Don't let guilt zap your pleasure. Your inner critic can rear its ugly head and try to convince you that you should be doing more or working on more productive things; or it may whisper some other nonsense that may cause you to feel like you are not doing enough or doing things right. If you and your family are happy with all you and they are doing, then it works and you have nothing to feel bad about.

996. Don't allow anyone else's comments to sway you. This is your life, and you have every right to choose how you want to live it. Only you have the power to let someone make you feel guilty or uncomfortable or wrong about your choices. Give yourself permission to live your life your way, and if that means someone is unhappy with your choices, they need to reconcile that themselves.

997. Stop comparing yourself to others. If you take notice of how long someone else's to-do list is or how many extracurricular activities their children are involved in, you are wasting time you could be using productively.

998. Try ignoring the Joneses by *not* keeping up with them. Just because someone else is doing something does not mean you have to. So you can opt out of lavish vacations, excess social events, and other things that are not a priority for you right now. Living a fulfilling life is about living based on your priorities, not trying to accumulate the most stuff.

999. Do not be envious of those who appear to have more time—they don't. Sometimes the grass just appears greener; others can look like they are getting more done or have more time, but this is not necessarily true. Whenever you feel like others are doing more, take a step back and regroup. When you focus on your side of the fence, you can get more done. And always remember that someone is looking at you and wondering how *you* get it all done.

1000. Only speak positively about time. Refrain from comments like "I'm so busy," "I'll never get this done," and "I don't have enough time." Instead, when you feel overwhelmed and in need of more time, say to yourself, "I have enough time." It is amazing how that change in your mindset can transform your whole attitude and minimize your stress level.

HAVE MORE TIME TODAY!

1. Pick one small change that will make a big difference and start today.
2. Put a new routine into action so you start and end your day on the right note.
3. Keep your time in balance by ensuring you always have one fun thing to do.

TRY THIS:

Do your own personal calculations to figure out how long tasks take you and when you need to start so you will end on time.

REPEAT AFTER ME:

"I prepare the night before, so my morning runs smoother."

Note from the Author

Dear Reader,

As I wrote this book, I was picturing you rushing through your day—overwhelmed, feeling behind, and generally stressed-out—and I wanted to provide you with effective and simple tips that would give you instant relief, because I don't want you to be so busy you miss out on the important stuff in your life.

I know that you can have more time in your day! I also know that there is plenty of time for you to do the things that you enjoy. I've just shared with you over a thousand ways to get more time out of your day. But please remember that all these great tips are just ideas until you put them into action. Your job is to get it going. You don't have to get it right; you just have to get it going!

Pick one idea, and try it out. Then add another and then another until you have regained control.

You can do this. Reclaiming your time is a process of all the little things you do, *not* one big change. So, start today by making one small adjustment. I am so excited to see how your life will change for the better once you have more control over your time.

I want to share with you some things I know for sure:

- You can't manage time; you can only manage yourself.
- Limiting your to-do list *before* you get your priorities straight is pointless.
- There will always be more to do. You will never be caught up.
- No one, without your permission, can make you feel guilty about how you choose to spend your time.
- If you don't learn to say "no" sometimes, you will never truly be happy.
- It comes down to making choices; you can't have it all.
- You can't do it all and do it all well.
- This is your life; it's not a dress rehearsal, and it goes by faster than you may think.
- There is always room for improvement, but you are doing a great job!

I hope you have enjoyed reading this book, and I invite you to stop by my website to get more ideas and inspiration. I'd love to hear from you, and I hope you will share your success story with me. Please contact my office toll free at 1-866-294-9900, or go to my website at www.jamienovak.com. Reminding you that life is not a dress rehearsal,

Jamie Novak

P.S. I've made every attempt to cover all the important areas, but if I missed a category that you'd like to see covered, I'd love to know about it.

P.P.S. I invite you to team up with a friend or a group of friends to start a Take Back Your Time group. I can even join you via speakerphone during one of your meetings. See the information in the back of this book or on my website at www.jamienovak.com.

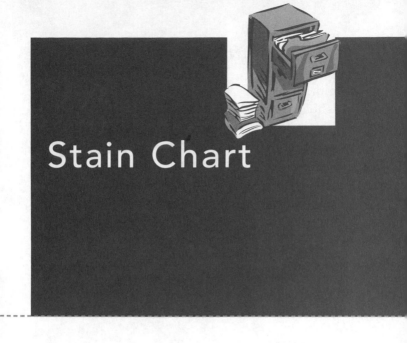

Stain Chart

GENERAL TIPS AND TRICKS

- Never dry a stained item in the dryer, since the stain will most likely become set in. Also, since the dry cleaning process can cause the stain to reappear, be sure to point out any spills to the dry cleaner even if you've already washed the garment yourself.
- When washing a stained area, rinse from the backside of the stain so you are not running the stain through the area front to back.
- Test your stain-removing remedy in an inconspicuous spot to ensure fabric compatibility before cleaning the entire stain.
- These are tried-and-true suggestions; however, you should always consult the manufacturer or your local dry cleaner for more thorough directions if the stained item is irreplaceable or made with a rare fabric.

STAIN-BUSTING TOOLS AND SUPPLIES

- Ammonia
- Dishpan (for soaking)
- Dishwashing liquid detergent
- Eyedropper (to help pinpoint the area when applying cleaning solutions)
- Hydrogen peroxide
- Lemon juice
- Mineral spirits (available at hardware stores and some grocery stores)
- Rubbing alcohol
- Store-bought stain remover
- Toothbrush (to thoroughly rub small areas)
- White vinegar

Barbeque Sauce: Scrape off as much excess as possible. Then use a store-bought stain remover. Follow up with white vinegar, if necessary, to remove any remaining color.

Blood: For a deep stain, soak in a cold water/saline solution. Follow with hydrogen peroxide to remove any color. Finish by washing the area with dishwashing detergent and then rinsing.

Butter: Start with a store-bought stain remover, and follow up with mineral spirits to remove any residue, if necessary.

Chocolate: Start with a store-bought stain remover and, if necessary, follow up with hydrogen peroxide directly on the stain to remove color.

Coffee: Use white vinegar to remove the color, and then follow up by rinsing with water.

Egg: For a deep stain, soak in a cold water/saline

solution. Follow with hydrogen peroxide to remove any color. Finish by using dishwashing detergent to wash the area; then rinse.

Grass: For a deep stain, soak in a cold water/saline solution. Follow with hydrogen peroxide to remove any color. Finish by using dishwashing detergent to wash the area and then rinse.

Gum: Use ice to freeze the gum. (You can even place the item in the freezer.) Once frozen, chip away at the gum. Rinsing with mineral spirits will remove any residue. If you have time, you can also take the item directly to the dry cleaners; they have a gum solvent that will do the job.

Ink (Ballpoint Pen): Spray hairspray directly onto the area, and then rinse out immediately with lukewarm water. If necessary, use dishwashing detergent as well.

Ink (Felt-tip Pen): Rinse area with rubbing alcohol, and then wash using dishwashing liquid.

Jam/Jelly/Preserves: Use rubbing alcohol to rinse the area. Then use white vinegar to remove the remaining color. Follow with dishwashing detergent to wash the area and rinse.

Juice: Use rubbing alcohol to rinse the area and then white vinegar to remove remaining color. Use dishwashing detergent to wash the area and rinse.

Ketchup: Scrape off as much excess as possible. Use a store-bought stain remover followed by white vinegar, if necessary, to remove any remaining color.

Lipstick: Start with a store-bought stain remover to remove the grease. Then flush the area with white vinegar to remove any remaining color.

Mayonnaise: Start with a store-bought stain remover, and follow up with mineral spirits to remove any residue, if necessary.

Mud: Allow it to dry so you can scrap off as much as possible, then soak in warm water and laundry detergent. Before drying, use white vinegar or hydrogen peroxide to remove any color from the area.

Mustard: Rinse the area thoroughly with ammonia, then wash with dishwashing detergent.

Oil: Start with a store-bought stain remover, and follow up with mineral spirits to remove any residue, if necessary.

Soy Sauce: Soak in warm water and dishwashing detergent. Then use hydrogen peroxide to remove any remaining color.

Tea: Rinse area with lemon juice to remove the color, and wash the garment as directed.

Tomato Sauce: Scrape off as much excess as possible. Use a store-bought stain remover followed by white vinegar, if necessary, to remove any remaining color.

Vegetable Juice: Use rubbing alcohol to rinse the area and white vinegar to remove the remaining color. Finish by washing the area with dishwashing detergent and then rinsing.

Vinaigrette: Start with a store-bought stain remover followed by white vinegar, if needed, to remove any remaining color.

Wax: Use ice to freeze the wax. (You can even place the item in the freezer.) Once frozen, chip away at the wax. Rinsing with mineral spirits will remove any residue. An alternative is to wrap the area in a brown paper bag and heat with an iron; the brown bag will soak up the melted wax.

Wine (Red): Treat with rubbing alcohol, followed by white vinegar to remove any remaining color.

Wine (White): Rinse thoroughly with cool water, and wash as directed.

Homemade Household Cleanser Recipes

These easy-to-mix cleansers are made of ingredients easily available at your local grocery store and will have your house sparkling in no time. Clearly label each container so you know what product is for what use. You might also want to write the recipe directly on the bottle, so you can refill it easily.

Many of these solutions contain vinegar, which is a great cleaning agent. Concerned about a vinegar smell being left behind after cleaning? Don't be. Once these solutions dry, the aroma disappears.

Gentle all-surface cleaner (For use on countertops, stove ranges, floors, toilet seats, refrigerator doors, shelves, and so much more.)

Mix 1 cup of white vinegar and 1 cup cool water in a spray bottle.

* For stubborn spots such as soap scum and water deposits, warm the solution and douse the area generously. Let stand for ten minutes before cleaning.

Strong all-surface cleaning solution
Mix 1 tablespoon of ammonia with 1 tablespoon clear laundry detergent with 2 cups cool water in a spray bottle.

Gentle scouring cleaner
(For bathtub rings, food residue in refrigerators, kitchen counters, and so much more.)

Find a clean and empty sprinkle-top Parmesan cheese container or sugar shaker. (Salt shaker holes are too small.) Fill the container with baking soda.

Sprinkle baking soda onto a damp sponge, and go to work.

Strong scouring paste cleaner
(For residue around faucets, tub, sink, soap scum, and much more.)

Make a paste using one part water and two parts baking soda. Then slather the paste onto tough-to-clean areas. Wait ten minutes and clean easily.

Toilet bowl cleaner
(Also for hard-to-clean mineral deposits or soap scum areas.)

To empty the toilet bowl, quickly pour a bucket of water into the bowl so the water is forced out. Then spray undiluted white vinegar all around the bowl. Scrub with your regular toilet brush, and use a pumice stone (yes, a pumice stone) to remove any hard-to-scrub rings.

Glass and shiny surface spray cleaner
(For windows, glass, chrome, ceramic tile, and much more.)

Mix 1 cup rubbing alcohol with 1 cup cool water and 1 tablespoon white vinegar in a spray bottle.

Strong soaking solution
(For showerheads and faucets with mineral deposits.)

Pour 1/2 cup of undiluted white vinegar into a plastic food storage bag, then attach the bag to the faucet or showerhead using a rubber band; be sure the item is soaking in the solution. Let stand for two to six hours, then rinse. Use an old toothbrush or baby bottle brush, if necessary, to clear the holes of any residue.

Support Groups

TAKE BACK YOUR TIME DISCUSSION GROUP

How would you like to meet with other people who are looking to save time and get organized? I invite you to create a Take Back Your Time discussion group. It's so easy. Just use this book as your guide. I like to make myself as available as I can, so once you create your group and have started reading my book, please let me know. I'd be delighted to call into your group's meeting and join you via speakerphone. I can share some of my best secrets from *1000 Best Quick and Easy Time-Saving Strategies* with the group, and you can tell me more about your situation. I would love to hear all about how you and your friends are implementing my solutions and making positive changes in your lives to make time for you and the things that are important to those you love. Just drop me an email at jamie@jamienovak.com or call toll free at 1-866-294-9900. I wish nothing but the very best for you.

Sincerely,
Jamie

ELEVEN SIMPLE STEPS TO CREATING YOUR OWN TAKE BACK YOUR TIME DISCUSSION GROUP

1. Locate at least one other person who struggles with getting everything done. (Consider your children's classmates' mothers, coworkers, friends, family, neighbors, friends or acquaintances from your house of worship, and other parents from your children's day care or extracurricular activities.)
2. Invite the person or people to the group.
3. Choose a place to meet. You might opt to rotate homes or meet in a café or library.
4. Pick a date and time to meet.
5. Decide how often the group will meet—weekly or monthly.
6. Be sure everyone reads chapter 1 of 1000 *Best Quick and Easy Time-Saving Strategies* before your first meeting.
7. At the first meeting, discuss the ten golden rules.
8. Consider designating one person per meeting as a timekeeper to ensure everyone has a chance to participate.
9. By the end of the meeting, be sure each person has stated a goal they plan to have accomplished

before the next meeting.

10. Assign the next chapter to be read before the next meeting.

11. Stay in touch between meetings to give each other support. Also, consider getting free online support through www.jamienovak.com.

CLUTTER CLUBS

If you are a professional organizer, coach, therapist, author, trainer, consultant, speaker, or clutter-prone person who wants to create a community of people looking to make positive changes in their lives by clearing their clutter and finding more time, then facilitating a Clutter Club might be right for you.

No previous experience is necessary, and you do not have to feel comfortable with public speaking. The Clutter Club is a fantastic, fully customizable way to connect with potential clients while creating a supportive community. If you'd like to offer such a program, but do not want to start from scratch, consider using the Clutter Club template and this book as your club resource. Contact the author to discuss how simple it can be to start a Clutter Club near you.

Looking for a Clutter Club to join? They are free and open to the public! Clubs meet monthly (some in person and some over the phone) and are great for getting ideas, tips, and inspiration! Check out www.jamienovak.com or call 1-866-294-9900 to locate a Clutter Club near you or for more information.

Index

D

daily organizing solutions, 369–75, 389
dates, 185
deadlines, 192; DIY projects, 416; pending papers and, 255,
256; procrastination and, 200, 209; spouses and, 187;
time-management objections and, 220–21; to-do lists
and, 49, 55; work-related, 88, 92
decision making, 27; calendars and, 39; clutter control and, 353,
361; holidays and birthdays, 401; moving and, 408; organizing solutions and, 387; procrastination and, 208, 210
decorations, 401–2
defier procrastination personality, 212
delays, planning for, 30
delegation: chores, 71; moving-related tasks, 405; work-
related, 88
deliveries, 137, 415
delivery services, 425
desks, work, 91, 93, 333–35, 345
desktop file box, 253–59
detail-challenged procrastination personality, 213
diaper bags, 180
digital cameras. *See* cameras
direct deposits, 269
Direct Marketing Association, 249–50
discipline, chronic lateness and, 198
dishwashers, 147, 149, 151, 160
distractions, 172, 223–27, 339
do-it-yourself (DIY), 413–18
donations, 251, 354, 358, 361, 406
doormats, 403
doors, 403
double-booking, 173
drawers: cleaning, 403; organizing solutions for, 379, 381,
382, 388. *See also* junk drawers
dressers, 78, 388
drink stations, 380
drop zones, 189
dry cleaning, 81, 453
dry cleaning kits, 81
dryers, 79, 453. *See also* laundry
drying racks, 82
dryness levels, in storage areas, 387
dusting, 153, 160

E

eating, 58, 87. *See also* cooking; meal planning; meals; pantry
eggs, hard-boiled, 116
egg separators, 118
electronic calendars, 45

296; meal planning, 104; moving-related, 406; organization and, 381; pending papers, 252, 253–54, 255, 256, 257; photos, 329; printing and, 262; shopping, 134; special needs children, 176; work desks and, 334

follow-ups, 22

food: cleaning and, 158; freezing, 120. *See also* cooking; eating; meal planning; meals

forms, 126, 171, 177, 181

freezers, organizing solutions for, 374

friends, 183, 185–89; email and, 283; fun and, 246; grocery shopping with, 113; holidays and birthdays, 396; meal planning and, 104; phone calls and, 320; social engagements and, 18; Take Back Your Time groups, 451, 464; time-management plan and, 21, 27

fun: chores and, 73; cleaning and, 145, 147; organizing solutions and, 389; procrastination and, 205–6; routines and, 439, 447; to-do lists and, 59

funnels, 118

G

garages: gardening and, 232; organizing solutions for, 386, 387, 389

garage sales, 362

garbage, 116, 159, 353, 416

gardening, 229, 231–38, 246

gardening tools and supplies, 232

gas tank, filling, 30

gift cards, 134

gifts: chores and, 72; consumable, 427; holidays and birthdays, 393–95, 399, 401, 418; hostess, 425; shopping and, 134, 135; traveling with, 409

gift-wrapping, 396–97, 402

glass spray cleaners, 461

glassware, organizing solutions for, 379

gloves: cleaning, 143; gardening, 234

goals, 29, 31, 53

groceries, bagging, 114

grocery shopping, 100, 109–14

grocery shopping lists, 110–12, 113

grouping, 51

guilt, 445

H

habits, procrastination and, 206

hair care, 61

hand-me-downs, 170

hanger organizers, 81, 383

hangers, 81, 82, 388, 423

hanging folders, 253–54, 255, 267–68

days, 402; meal planning and, 104; moving and, 407; organizing solutions and, 382; pantry shelves, 374; pending papers, 255; return address, 126; special event files and, 418; special needs children and, 176

lateness, chronic, 195–201

Laundromats, 76

laundry, 75–83; cleaning and, 159; exercise and, 244; stains and, 453; vacations and, 411

laundry areas/rooms, 83

laundry baskets, 77

laundry chutes, 83

laundry detergent, 460

laundry sorters, 79

lawn care. *See* gardening

leashes, for pets, 235

leaving station, 125, 138

letter openers, 250, 275

lids, 380

linen closets, 80

lint rollers, 237, 402, 403

lists: chores, 71; errands, 126; grocery shopping, 110–12, 113; home repairs, 72; master, 52; mental, 50; rewriting, 52, 55, 126, 186; spouses and, 186; time-management objections and, 221; work-related, 88; writing, 16. *See also* to-do lists

litter boxes, 237

living room cleaning, 156

living space, organizing solutions for, 377–83, 389

login information, online, 136

lost-and-found bins, 83, 189

luggage, 410–11

lunch breaks, 87

M

magazines, sorting through, 155

mail, 249–59, 275; cleaning and, 155–56, 160; moving and, 405; organizing solutions for, 371; traveling and, 411

mailing lists, 249, 251

makeup, 60–61, 153

Market Day, 110

master lists, 52

maybe boxes, 361, 408

meal planning, 99–107, 121. *See also* cooking

meals, 97; cooking, 115–21; grocery shopping, 109–14; meal planning and pantry, 99–107; rating, 101. *See also* cooking

measuring cups, 119

medications, for pets, 236

meetings, 337–39, 345

mending, 80, 159

mental clutter, 225

organization systems, maintaining, 363–65

organizing solutions, 367; everyday, 369–75, 389; living space, 377–83, 389; paperwork, 424; storage space, 385–89

organizing supplies, 360

ovens, 117, 160

over-cleaning, 145

over-commitment, 199, 426

P

packing: evening routines and, 432; moving and, 407, 408; vacations, 424

pantry, 99–107, 374

paper clips, 42

paper-towel holders, 158

paperwork, 247; appointments and, 181; bill-paying, filing, and record-keeping, 267–75; chronic lateness and, 200; clutter control and, 352; organizing, 424; pending, 253–59; pet-related, 236; saving, 261–65, 275; vacations and, 418; volunteering and, 433; work processes and, 342. See also forms; mail

par levels, 39, 360

parents, 163; children, 165–73; infants, 179–81; special needs children, 175–77. See also children; family

parking, 127–28

parties, 394–97, 407, 418

partners, grocery shopping with, 113. See also family

passwords, online, 136, 285

PDAs, 297–309

pen cups, organizing solutions for, 379

pending paperwork, 253–59

people pages, 92

people pleaser procrastination personality, 215

perfectionist procrastination personality, 211

personal quotient, 31

perspective, 28

pets, 229, 231–38, 243, 246

phone headsets, 318

phone messages, 318

phones, 223, 313–20, 330, 435. See also conference calls; contact information

phone tag, 319

photos, 311, 323–30; clutter control and, 354; holidays and birthdays, 398–99, 401; shopping and, 425

physical activity. See exercise

pick-up services, 425

pillowcases. See bedding

planners, 45–48, 50, 65

planning, 26, 49–56, 196, 210. See also meal planning

responsibility, 13, 32–33
rest, 58
restarting, 207
restaurants: online menus and, 105; take-out menus and, 104–5
return address labels, 126
rewards, 205–6, 441
rewriting, 42, 44, 52, 55, 186
ringtones, 316
Rolodex, 285, 333
routines: children-related, 173; chronic lateness and, 199; completing, 15; distractions and interruptions, 227; evening, 62, 65, 79, 429–37, 447; exercise and, 243; gardening-related, 233; morning, 59, 429–37, 447; new, 447; rethinking, 26; stress management, 63; timing, 14; work, 88, 91. See also time-management plan
rubbing alcohol, 461
rugs, washing, 76
rules, chronic lateness and, 197

S

safety, for DIY projects and repairs, 416
sales, grocery shopping and, 112
sandwich-making items, organizing solutions for, 377
schedules/scheduling, 37–48; breaks from, 62; children and, 165, 173; chores, 69; exercise, 245; holidays and birthdays, 401; homework, 436; laundry and, 76; photo organization, 328; time-management plan and, 444; to-do lists and planning, 49, 50; work, 88, 90. See also appointments; calendars; planners
school papers, 167, 176
scouring cleaners, 460
scrapbooks, 325
screening: phone calls, 318; visitors, 93
search engines, 293–94
seasonal clothing, 78, 385, 402
self-discipline, 198
set-up, 7–11
sewing, 239–41
sheds, 232
sheets. See bedding
shelves: cleaning solutions for, 459; organizing solutions for, 374, 382, 386
shoe holders, 240
shoes: cleaning and, 141; organizing solutions for, 370–71; packing for travel, 409
shopping, 133–38, 393. See also grocery shopping
shopping bags, 145, 378
"should," 28
showerheads, cleaning solutions for, 461
showers, cleaning, 424

T

About the Author

Photo © Sumaya/2005

Jamie Novak, also known as the Clutter Whisperer, is a dynamic speaker, television personality, and best-selling author who, in a humorous and heart-warming way, inspires people to calm the chaos of clutter and live a life based on their priorities. Novak provides real solutions for those living in the real world. She promises never to suggest impractical solutions.

A visionary, Novak created a unique business model for those in need of help, to support them while changing their habits. Clutter Clubs are nationally franchised discussion and support groups facilitated by professional organizers and open to the public at no charge.

Additionally, Novak works closely with those going into the professional organizing professions, training professional organizers in the Jamie Novak philosophy and methods. Instead of simply showing clients how to contain clutter, she shares with them simple techniques for sustainable change by getting to the root of the issue.

In her previous book, *1000 Best Quick and Easy Organizing Secrets*, Novak offers over one thousand easy-to-implement, no-fail solutions for clearing clutter in every area of your life. Her trademark three-step process is highlighted in this portable and easy-to-read book.

Novak has been a featured expert on HGTV's *Mission: Organization*. She is the resident organizing expert for www.ivillage.com, delivers a regular segment on *The World According to Judith*, and is frequently featured on national radio shows like *The Dr. Laura Show*.

Her articles can be found in numerous print publications, such as *Decorating Solutions* and online at iVillage, and she is quoted in such national magazines as *Woman's Day*. She is also a top-rated expert on www.allexperts.com. As a nationally sought-after presenter, Novak inspires audiences at regional and national speaking engagements, such as National Organization of Mothers of Twins Clubs (NOMOTC) Convention and the Mahwah Library. Additionally, she also conducts corporate seminars for clients such as Merck and the New Jersey Chapter of the National Association of Woman Business Owners (NJAWBO), which help employees conquer disorder in the workplace.

Earning a degree in communications, Novak graduated from Union College. She currently divides her time between her main office in Scotch Plains, New Jersey, and her west coast branch in Palmdale, California.

If you'd like to share a success story or submit your favorite tip, view other free resources, or get an answer to your biggest time or clutter challenge, visit www.jamienovak.com.

Jamie challenges you to organize from the outside in. Once you gain control of your stuff, step back and watch what happens! To get your free copy of Jamie's latest e-zine, *The Clutter Challenge*, or to find out more about her, visit her website today.